AHEAD OF HIS TIME
SELECTED SPEECHES OF GUNNAR DYBWAD

Edited by

Mary Ann Allard, PhD
McCormack Institute for Public Affairs
University of Massachusetts Boston

Anne M. Howard, PhD
Fitchburg State College

Lee E. Vorderer, MA
Eunice Kennedy Shriver Center
for Mental Retardation, Inc.

Alice I. Wells, PhD
University of Maryland

David L. Braddock, PhD
Books and Research Monographs Editor

AAMR
American Association on Mental Retardation

© 1999 by the American Association on Mental Retardation

Published by
American Association on Mental Retardation
444 North Capitol Street, NW, Suite 846
Washington, DC 20001-1512

The points of view herein are those of the authors and do not necessarily represent the official policy or opinion of the American Association on Mental Retardation. Publication does not imply endorsement by the editor, the Association, or its individual members.

Printed in the United States of America.

Library of Congress Cataloging-in-Publication Data
Dybwad, Gunnar.
    Ahead of his time: selected speeches of Gunnar Dybwad/edited by Mary Ann Allard…[et al.].
        p. cm.
    Includes bibliographical references.
    ISBN 0-940898-61-6
    1. Mentally handicapped—United States. 2. Mentally handicapped—Civil rights—United States. 3. Mentally handicapped—Deinstitutionalization—United States.
I. Allard, Mary Ann. II. Title.
HV3006.A4D93   1999
362.3'0973—dc21   99-15915
                                                                                       CIP

Dedication

People influence one another. When we're small, our influences are our families; then our friends take a preeminent role in helping us set our directions. Eventually we become more selective, and we have to look outside our closest circles for advice and guidance.

Some of us are lucky, though, and we find the guidance close to home. The editors of this book shared in having as guides several very special people. One is Gunnar Dybwad, and readers will see why as they come to know him through his speeches. Another is his wife, Rosemary, who through her gentle hand and vision led each of us to thinking about the lives of people with disabilities. Rosemary's influence is international; we are four of the fortunate many who knew and loved her.

Finally, Anne Howard, Alice Wells, and Lee Vorderer had the remarkable joy of sharing the creation of this book with Mary Ann Allard. Her sense of what mattered, her thoughtful analysis, her sense of humor, and her kindness infused every decision we made about what to include and how to structure these remarkable pieces.

Her death in July 1998 leaves the rest of us to carry on the project, and we dedicate this work to her memory:
Mary Ann Allard.

Table of Contents

Preface vii
Introduction by Allen C. Crocker ix
    Chapter 1. "The Lasting Verities" 1

PART 1: The Words We Use 3
    Editors' Introduction 5
    Chapter 2. Our Concepts Will Affect the
    Development of Children 7
        Some Sources of Confusion 8
        Levels of Intelligence 8
    Chapter 3. Care for the Severely Retarded in
    the United States 11
    Chapter 4. Whom Do We Call Mentally
    Retarded? 17

PART 2: Human Potential, Human Rights 23
    Editors' Introduction 25
    Chapter 5. Rights and Duties 27
    Chapter 6. The Concept of Normalization 31
    Chapter 7. Ethical and Legal Problems
    in Rehabilitation and Medicine 35
        Infants With Birth Defects 35
        Parents' Role in Decision Making 36
        Decisions and Facts 37
        Considering Potential 38
        The Phillip Becker Case 39
        The Justin Clark Case 39
    Chapter 8. Basic Legal Aspects in Providing
    Medical, Educational, Social, and Vocational
    Help to the Mentally Retarded 41
        The Right to Education 43
        The Right to Work 45
        The Right to an Appropriate Place
        to Live 46
        The Mentally Retarded Person as a
        Citizen 46
        The Mentally Retarded Child's Right to
        Live With His Family 46
        The Right to Medical Care 47
        The Rights in Balance 47

PART 3: Early Intervention 49
    Editors' Introduction 51
    Chapter 9. Why Does Early Intervention
    Come So Late? 53
    Chapter 10. The Mentally Handicapped
    Child Under Five 57
        Case Finding 57
        Services 58
            Parent Education 58
            Counseling 59
            Psychotherapy 59
        Practical Help 59
            Family Help 60
            Guidance in Child Development 60
            Home Help 61
            Short-Term Care 61
            Baby-Sitting 62
        Pediatric Care 62
            Down Syndrome 63
            Speech Problems 63
        Lessening Dependence 63
            Nursery Schools 64
            Who Am I? The Self-Concept 64
        Physical Fitness 64
        Label the Services, Not the Child 65
    Chapter 11. What Went Wrong? 67
    Chapter 12. The Rediscovery of the Family 71

PART 4: The Role of Professionals 75
   Editors' Introduction 77
      Chapter 13. Toward Human Rights for the Mentally Retarded: A Challenge to Social Action 79
      Chapter 14. The "Medical Model" 83
      Chapter 15. Parents and Professionals 85

PART 5: Deinstitutionalization 89
   Editors' Introduction 91
      Chapter 16. Beginnings and Endings: The Quality of Life for Young and Old 93
      Chapter 17. The Undeveloped Resource at the Edge of Change 95
      Chapter 18. A Society Without Institutions? 99

PART 6: Adult Citizens in the Community 105
   Editors' Introduction 107
      Chapter 19. The Mentally Retarded Adult's Place in Society 109
      Chapter 20. International Developments in the Social Rehabilitation of the Handicapped 113
      Chapter 21. Normalization and Integration—Shifting Empires 117
         Nine Exemplary Shifts 117
         Effects of the Changing Policies 121
      Chapter 22. Normalization and Its Impact on Social and Public Policy 123
         Normalization and Community Integration 124
      Chapter 23. Access to Work 127

PART 7: Advocacy and Empowerment 129
   Editors' Introduction 131
      Chapter 24. We Have to Fight 133
      Chapter 25. Lest We Forget 139
         Psychiatry Neglects Retardation 140
         Heavy Institutional Investment 141
         Other Factors Inhibit Change 142
         Glossing Over Horrors 142
         Harsh Words in a Federal Report 143
         "Plan" Is an Important Step 143
      Chapter 26. Self-Determination: Influencing Public Policy 145
      Chapter 27. The Revolutionary Vision Unfolds 151
      Chapter 28. Transitions in Action: Impact on the Planning Process 155
         Parents 156
         International Variation 157
         Rights of Mentally Retarded People 158
      Chapter 29. Using the Courts 161
      Chapter 30. "A Debt of Gratitude" 163
      Chapter 31. From Feeblemindedness to Self-Advocacy 167
      Chapter 32. Leadership in Self-Advocacy 171
      Chapter 33. Societal Perspectives: Where Do We Go From Here? 173

Biographical Sketch of Gunnar Dybwad 177
References 179

Preface

This book is not intended to be a history of mental retardation policy or practice. Rather, it is designed to illustrate how one person, who is able to think and articulate his thoughts clearly and who is willing to speak out when necessary, can influence an entire field of policy and practice. We reviewed more than 200 of Gunnar Dybwad's speeches, before deciding on the 33 in this volume. We sought to include speeches that were particularly insightful, and those that challenged prevailing thinking of the time. We included speeches that span the wide range of disability issues Gunnar has studied over the years and those that trace his own growth and change. These speeches reflect Gunnar's international perspective, and they reveal his solid grounding in the lives and wisdom of people with mental retardation and their families. We also selected speeches for their ability to be appreciated as written documents. Some of our original choices suffered without the passion and vitality of Gunnar's voice and delivery and were ultimately omitted. Finally, we selected speeches that remind us how far we have come, and those that, despite the passage of time, continue to provide guidance for the future.

This sample of Gunnar's speeches is organized into seven topical sections. Each section is preceded by a short introduction written following a conversation with Gunnar on that particular topic. It is noteworthy that he could recall the content of each speech and speak eloquently on each topic, without any preparation. And truly remarkable that he could do so at the age of 89.

These introductions are intentionally brief and reflect Gunnar's desire not to draw conclusions for the reader. Rather, our intention is to highlight key ideas and provide a context for the speeches that follow.

We have chosen not to alter the language of the original speeches. Rather, we have preserved it as a signal of the thinking of that period. Each speech includes information about when and where it was originally delivered. For speeches that have been published elsewhere, publishing information is provided. To the fullest extent possible, we have sought to provide complete references. It is important to remember that speeches do not typically have written references!

As with most collaborative ventures, this project would not have been possible without the contributions of others. We are extremely grateful for the encouragement and assistance of Dr. Gunnar Dybwad. He has been extraordinarily patient and generous with his time and materials. Jim O'Brien, from the University of Massachusetts—Boston, provided an objective viewpoint and expert editorial support as we worked to shape the speeches into an organized whole. The editors also gratefully acknowledge the critical support of Dr. Marty Krauss and the Starr Center for Mental Retardation at the Heller School, Brandeis University. Finally, special thanks go to Dr. David Braddock, AAMR Books and Monographs Editor, for his enthusiasm and his assistance with the publication of this work.

Compiling this selection of Gunnar Dybwad's speeches has been both a challenge and a labor of love. It has taken us far longer than any of us could have predicted and has left us more appreciative of Gunnar's work than ever before. Each of us has known Gunnar for 20 years or more and can recount story after story of how his wisdom and friendship have influenced our thinking and our work. We feel extraordinarily lucky to have had Gunnar as a teacher and guide, and this book grew out of our love and respect for him. It is our hope that by publishing this sampling of Gunnar's speeches, others will benefit from Gunnar's foresight and insight over the past 35 years. Enjoy!

Introduction

Allen C. Crocker
Children's Hospital
Boston, Massachusetts

Through the years we have had the words of Gunnar Dybwad in numerous ways. Many of those ways are less structured, such as the bountiful ones we remember as he has led discussions, provided commentary at board or committee meetings, made observations while carrying out significant visits to all manner of programs, given arm-on-the-shoulder advice in friendship, offered salutes and tributes at gatherings of faithful friends, and spoken strategic testimony at turning points in public policy determination. Less often we have had his words in papers and other written materials. But then there have been the speeches. Thank God for the speeches—passionate, no-nonsense, historically rich, always instructive, and usually 45 minutes long! It is a cause for celebration that the editors of this book have tracked down the speeches, and in so doing have secured a priceless core of Gunnar's wisdom.

Gunnar is a gentle but commanding figure who has guided the modern evolution of the field of studies and services in mental retardation. By example, by support, and by ideas he has helped all of us, one by one and by hundreds, to get a broader and deeper understanding of this territory, to feel more certain, and to behave in a more resolved fashion

Gunnar began his studies in Europe, in law. His early work in the United States was in juvenile delinquency and child welfare. In 1957 he became the second executive director of the National Association for Retarded Children, and the die was cast. He made critically important contributions to the preparations for the President's Panel on Mental Retardation in the Kennedy administration, the beginning of contemporary affirmations in our field. In the 40 years since, he has been a part of all the major components of the mental retardation scene. Particularly gratifying assignments have involved work with the United Nations, the World Health Organization, and the International League of Societies for Persons With Mental Handicap. He has been a member of virtually every commission, council, and planning group of note in the field. This feat was assisted by his remarkable capacity to take cat naps during meetings at low points in the activity. He has been the recipient of uncountable awards. Gunnar became especially well known as professor of human development, and director of the Starr Center for Mental Retardation, in the Heller School at Brandeis University. There he was the steward of many generations of fortunate graduate students and the host to an endless series of seminars, rallies, and task forces.

One could note that work in mental retardation was and is distinctive and uniquely engaging. For professionals and families alike there is generally a spirit of outreach, sharing, and helping. New pathways are continually being built, and there are victories on the road. It was like a revolution waiting to happen. Coconspirators feel a warm and special fellowship. For this kind of reform and joining, Gunnar is an absolute natural.

Most compelling for Gunnar, perhaps, has been his concerns with access (including environmental), social equity, and self-advocacy. The material of the speeches in this book will tell those stories. Gunnar has a prodigious recollection of the comrades and events in the world of mental retardation, and it can be assured that none of his allies has forgotten him either. In the simplest term, he has been a teacher. But beyond that, he has been a theorist, a lover, a confederate, and a friend. The Rosemary F. Dybwad International Fellowships enlarge the vision of young workers. The Howe Library sustains the study of believers of all ages. His local and international travel does not cease, and his hospitality is immense.

It has been heartening to watch Gunnar find amazement and some peace with his senior citizen status. This was best exemplified by his joy at the arrival of his two great grandchildren. Son Peter, in Berkeley, and daughter Susan, in Nashville, have brought great pride, as have the five wonderful grandchildren. His beloved partner, Rosemary, 58 years his wife, gave him life (and the garden).

It will be a treasure to have this book. It is part of the movement. It shows Gunnar as a commentator, critic, and prophet. Also he can be seen as an historian who has remained young. Gunnar Dybwad has brought nurturance to us all. It is exciting to find so many of his lessons now implemented and so many of his hopes realized.

Chapter 1
"The Lasting Verities"

Concluding remarks upon receiving an honorary degree of Doctor of Humane Letters from Temple University, Philadelphia, February 1977

And now that I can look back to almost 50 years of work in what we call the field of human services, where do I see the lasting verities, which have increasingly fashioned my approach to serving persons with a handicap?

1. In dealing with the problem of human growth and development, one should never say "never"—there is always change, the dynamics of which so far have not become clear to scientific exploration. No one can predict as a human being is born, where the limits of that person's growth and development will be. I reject and resent the arrogance of bureaucratic and professional workers who predetermine another person's potential.

2. One may continue trying to apply measurements to intellectual functioning, adaptive behavior, and emotional maturity, but the inherent dignity of any human being, no matter how severely disabled, cannot be quantitatively assessed, and to do so in the name of ethics (as has been tried) is a mockery of that term.

3. In searching for solutions to human problems, I am more and more impressed with the overwhelming importance of one's personalized environment—for the child, the family; for the adult, in addition his home, his own living space. Thus, home support looms ever larger on my list of priorities.

4. This leads me to underline one point of wisdom from Lewis Carroll's *Alice in Wonderland*. I have often said that all administrators should have this book on their desk for easy reference. You may recall that Alice asked the Queen, "Where shall I begin?" and the Queen answered her, "Begin at the beginning." In the field of handicap…we most certainly have failed badly in that respect. Early intervention is particularly essential for persons with severe disabilities who require long-term care.

5. After 10 years of teaching doctoral students (whose knowledge and skills often awe me), I recognize that frequently we create or exasperate problems by pompous words. The King's English—simple, direct language in our communications—must be more recognized as a valuable tool. Along with it comes my faith in what Adolph Meyer, the distinguished psychiatrist and cofounder of our mental health movement, called the science of disciplined common sense. Along with it must also be mentioned the admonition Edgar Doll, pioneer in clinical psychology and father of the *Vineland Social Maturity Scale*, addressed to his students in his last years: Don't *over*estimate the value of so-called objective tests and don't *under*estimate the value of your own structured observations. In other words, I have come to look upon a lot of ongoing research with a very jaundiced

eye, because I am convinced that, to a considerable extent, the facts upon which the research is supposedly based are skewed by the fact finders' biases.

6. Much of my most significant learning in the field of disability I owe to parents of children with handicaps. But more and more I am convinced that we must listen to a far greater degree to the individuals with handicaps. For a long time we thought those with more severe disability could not learn; now we know we did not yet know how to teach. Similarly, what we call the inability of persons with severe handicaps to communicate may well be our ineptness in listening. So we must learn to listen, and while this is not easy for those whose hearing is going sour, try we must.

And now let me thank again Temple University for the great honor they have bestowed on me, and thank you all for your presence here. It is a great evening for the Dybwads.

Part 1

The Words We Use

Editors' Introduction to Part 1

That humans are a judgmental species is indisputable; what deserves serious thought are the bases upon which people make judgments. First impressions are particularly powerful informers of judgment, as are the words used to describe or label. Over the past century, the labels that have been applied to people with disabilities have changed. For *many years* the manner in which professionals referred to people with mental retardation enabled society to pay little respect to the humanity of those people. Terms such as *feebleminded* and *idiot* were the accepted clinical terms, and *mentally retarded* or *mentally ill* were used in professional writing and in common parlance. Such terms often were preceded by *the*, reinforcing the notion that people with retardation were clinical subjects instead of people and could be considered collectively rather than as individuals. The labels influenced society's judgments about people with retardation.

Dr. Dybwad began his work at a time when the term *feebleminded* was used as professional language in texts and journals, and this was soon replaced by the term *mentally retarded*. As he came to know people about whom these terms were used, Dr. Dybwad became impressed with the artificial nature of these words. When scientific terms are used in common parlance, it is implied that such terms are appropriate. When these terms are derogatory, the perception of "appropriateness" leads to an overall negative view of the people to whom they refer. Negative physical treatment may soon follow, and the terms and treatment become an interlocking problem. "First, you put on a label, and then subject your thinking to that label, and it becomes a vicious circle" (Dybwad, personal communication, August 1998).

In the speeches that follow, Dr. Dybwad discusses the effects of these negative terms on the lives of the individuals involved, on the systems that provide services, and on the expectations that are engendered in others.

Chapter 2
Our Concepts Will Affect the Development of Children

Excerpt from 1964 report, "The Dynamics of Retardation," presented for the Miriam Home for the Exceptional, Montreal, 1963

A great many of the "facts" which are still associated by many people with mental retardation are a result of our ideas about what these individuals could *not* do. Terman said: "All who test below 70 IQ by the Stanford revision of the Binet-Simon scale should be considered feeble-minded" (1916, p. 85). So we considered those who scored below 70 on the tests as mentally deficient and placed them in institutions and, indeed, once so placed, they functioned, after a while, as though they were mentally deficient.

This "closed system" is illustrated very well in what is known as the global concept of intelligence on which most intelligence tests were developed. Since this concept was the basic assumption underlying the test, any item which did not have a high correlation with the whole test was eliminated. All future research using this test could not help but support that basic assumption.

Another example of the type of error often repeated is the failure to distinguish between the type of service needed and prognosis. If a child was thought to need "custodial care" or was a "crib case" at admission, this became the prognosis. The very term *crib case* implied this child was incapable of being outside a crib—so nobody bothered to help these youngsters to start moving about.

Thus, the way in which we treat the individual considered to be mentally retarded will have a definite effect upon his development. If our concept of mental retardation is static, if we think these individuals are incurable, if we treat them as though they are also morally deficient, in addition—then we can predict, with a high degree of reliability, that their functioning will definitely be limited and their ability to deal with moral problems will certainly be deficient.

However, if we expect a great deal more of them, and consequently provide the training, the opportunities, and the encouragement by which our expectations can be realized, then there is a good possibility that these individuals will function at a much higher level than had ever been anticipated in the past.

If it is recognized that each individual is different, within his own pattern of skills and weaknesses, then we can build on the skills and try to strengthen his weaknesses. This will require a different approach in each individual.

The concept of the changing individual points up the necessity for assessment and reassessment. The idea that once we have given the individual a number, an IQ, he is then "pegged" for life, fails to recognize the fact that individuals do change over a period of time. We need to make much more careful analysis of an individual's skills and weaknesses, and we need to evaluate the effectiveness of the education, training, and treatment which has been initiated as the result of previous findings.

Each individual lives in a society and in a family, whether this family is the one into which he is born or the one into which he is placed. The attitudes of the people who are around him each day are the attitudes he eventually takes on as his own. The individual who is met with fear continuously begins to think of himself as someone to be feared. The individual who is met with pity continuously soon comes to think of himself as someone to be pitied. The individual who is warmly received comes to think of himself as a friendly person who is well-liked.

The concept that we have about mental retardation will affect the way in which we approach the individuals who are so classed. This, in turn, will affect the way in which the individuals who come under our care will develop. Therefore it is important that we keep the individual in focus rather than the diagnosis. The medical care of the mentally retarded furnishes another example. All too often the "static" concept of the past led physicians to consider as inevitable the physical disabilities and ailments of the more severely retarded. As a result, there was often a quite unnecessary deterioration which then again was seen as substantiating the original premise that with these individuals therapeutic and ameliorative steps did not have to be considered.

In recent years most remarkable success was achieved when in some progressive institutions the medical and nursing staffs began an aggressive program of physical therapy with patients who were both physically and mentally severely handicapped. This new treatment approach did not only result, in many cases, in distinct physical improvement. Rather, these patients became more responsive and their general performance level began to improve.

Some Sources of Confusion

When psychological measurement is used for classification, there is a tendency to describe a child with a certain mental age as being just like a child of that chronological age. It is rather easy to see that this is not the case, since no 5-year-olds are of adult size. Although a retarded person with a mental age of 5 might be an adult, such a person should hardly be treated like a 5-year-old.

Another common error is to group individuals for one purpose and then to maintain this grouping even though the purpose is no longer the same. The reasons for classification change with age and the criteria for classification must also change. Thus, terminology appropriate for children may not be appropriate for adults. For example, the terms *educable* and *trainable* are widely in use for purposes of schooling, but this same classification is inappropriate in dealing with adults. As set forth earlier, the factors differentiating between assignments to classes on the educable and trainable levels are different from the factors determining success in an adult workshop or employment situation.

It is important to be rather flexible with any classification system—that the classification be used only for the purpose of grouping individuals for services, and that there is recognition of the limitations of the classification. Thus, it should always be possible to move a child from one group to another as one sees him function within the group or sees his functioning change over a period of time.

Levels of Intelligence

The traditional three-level classification is at least 100 years old, since Duncan, as early as 1860, described simpletons, imbeciles, and idiots (Duncan, 1860). Now, 100 years later, the American Association on Mental Deficiency has suggested a new definition of mental retardation, along with a new classification of four levels—mild, moderate, severe, and profound mental retardation—as formulated in 1959 (with a subsequent editorial revision in 1960). The American Association on Mental Deficiency definition is as follows: "Mental retardation refers to subaverage general intellectual functioning which originates during the developmental period and is associated with impairment in adaptive behavior" (Heber, 1959).

In combining the criteria of measured intelligence and impairment in adaptive behavior (i.e., the ability to comply with the expectations society requires the average person to fulfill), this new classification allows for a better balanced judgment and is a more discriminatory tool, particularly in planning for and working with those with a greater degree of retardation.

The mildly retarded, delineated approximately by a Binet IQ of 53 to 68, are by far the largest group, representing somewhat less than 90% of all the retarded. With special education and training, the majority of the mildly retarded can manage to be self-sufficient, if not self-maintaining, in adult life.

The moderately retarded, with a Binet IQ range from 36 to 52, comprise about 6% of the retarded population. It is this group that has astonished even the most experienced mental retardation practitioners by their capacity for achievement. Once considered "uneducable" (and, indeed, many psychologists, physicians, and educators still cling to this view), many of them now attend public school classes, later profit from simple work training, and work well in a sheltered environment, being able to use public transportation.

The severely retarded constitute about 3.5% of the total group. With a Binet IQ range from 20 to 35, they can learn self-care to a large measure and, unless physical conditions interfere, quite a few of them can engage in useful activity. (Both institutional and community facilities report their experience with this group progressively becoming more favorable.)

The profoundly retarded are the smallest group, accounting for about 1.5% of the retarded, with a Binet IQ below 20; with their great dependency on 24-hour care, most of them are in institutions. However, even in this group many respond to training on a minimal basis and to write them off as "custodial" or "crib" cases is to deny them the dignity and opportunity to develop and improve, which must not be denied any human being, no matter how limited.

Chapter 3
Care for the Severely Retarded in the United States

Excerpt from a presentation at the Third International Seminar on Special Education, Bad Harzburg, Germany, September 1966

In the field of education, there has been rather wide adoption internationally of the terms *educable* and *trainable*. You are all, of course, acquainted with these terms, and I hope some of you will agree that they were a very bad choice indeed. Presumably, *educable* was to be a higher level, designating at least a partial academic connotation, while *trainable* was to indicate a lower level of nonacademic, practical instruction.

The first objection one has to raise is that this is not in keeping with general language usage where we often speak of nursery school *education* on the one hand, and medical or legal *training* on the other.

The second, more serious, objection is that while presumably this dual terminology represented a differential in the mode of *schooling*, we instead bestowed this label on the *children*. Instead of saying that John was in a class on the trainable level, we said that John was trainable. All of you know what the result has been in practice. We find that we have in educable classes some children who are designated "trainable" and in trainable classes some children who are educable. All of this has developed, of course, from the fact that no sooner had it been decided to have this functional educational differentiation between an educable and a trainable level, when these terms were applied as "modern" psychometric terms, with a convenient, though hardly rational, dividing line at IQ 50, no matter what test was used. In other words, all children with a Binet IQ between 50 and 70 or 75 were called educable; all children with a Binet IQ below that, down to 25 or 30, were called trainable. Thus, the inevitable happened—since obviously not all school-age children with a Binet IQ between 25 or 30 and 50 are capable of adjusting in a classroom situation, there are "trainable" children who are not admitted to classes for the trainable.

This terminological puzzle reflects acutely the confused thinking that has plagued us in the United States as far as education of the mentally retarded is concerned, and I have dwelt on these facts which are, of course, known to you, because I want to underline them from an international point of view. Although the World Health Organization's (WHO) Technical Report *The Mentally Subnormal Child* 12 years ago, in 1954, pointed out that real difficulties are encountered in attempting to differentiate education from mere training, and all the criteria of trainability are applicable also to educability, many countries we have visited are still planning the education of the mentally retarded along the dichotomy between educable and trainable.

As was already pointed out in the 1954 report of WHO, there are of course distinct differences in the educational capacity of mentally retarded children, but it is a matter of degree, a sliding scale, and not a sharp division between two separate approaches to schooling.

In turning now to specific developments in the United States, I shall report first on the public school programs, then on vocational training and workshops and provisions for those not even eligible for these two programs. I will then report on residential care, special services and facilities for the adult retarded, and conclude with a report on new developments which are largely a result of the impact of President Kennedy's Panel on Mental Retardation.

Between 30,000 and 35,000 moderately and severely retarded children are attending at this time in the United States public school classes on the "trainable" level. This large number is proof of the fact that education of these children has now been accepted, from a national point of view, as a responsibility of the public schools. The first such classes were started more than half a century ago. St. Louis introduced them in 1941; New York City has had so-called "low IQ classes" for children below an IQ of 50 since 1929, and many other large cities, though often only on an experimental basis, also introduced such programs.

In 1952, when the U.S. Office of Education published its pamphlet entitled *The Forward Look—The Severely Retarded Child Goes to School*, it acknowledged that it was still a matter of debate whether provision of school services for this type of child was a function of the public schools or of the public welfare agencies. Ten years later this was no longer an open question, and the Office of Education issued a booklet, *Education of the Severely Retarded Child—Classroom Programs*, taking it for granted that this had become an obligation of the public schools. In the intervening years, however, we experienced in the United States a bitter controversy among educators and between educators and the Associations for Retarded Children.

While much credit is due to the progressive administrators of these large city school systems which had introduced classes for the children on this lower level, the total number of children served was very small indeed. Therefore when, around 1950, in the United States as in so many other countries, parents of retarded children began to band together to find ways to overcome the social isolation and educational neglect of their children, they pursued two lines of attack. They organized private classes themselves as best they could and with as much professional help as they were able to attract, and, at the same time, put pressure on the state authorities to extend the still very limited provisions for the mildly retarded children to include a much wider range of more severely handicapped children.

Not only tradition-bound school administrators but also some very outstanding and progressive leaders in special education of the physically handicapped violently opposed such a broadening of the education base. They insisted that education was a privilege which could be extended only to those capable of returning "value received" to the community, only to those able to live an independent life. Let me quote from a statement of one of these leaders of special education: "Education, as defined by Dewey and others, demands the ability to generalize; to reason and make judgments; to remember and to form new concepts out of previous learning; to solve problems; to abstract and to deal with abstractions; to utilize language concepts. Obviously, the severely retarded child lacks these abilities." This statement is a good example of a problem that plagued us very much in the United States in those days and that is certainly still encountered today in many countries. A prominent educator or psychologist makes categorical statements about the incapacity of the mentally retarded that give the appearance of scientific findings but are made without any adequate study or clinical observation.

Today of course, as I shall bring out later, we know that moderately and severely retarded children are certainly capable of achieving, to a varying degree, some of these intellectual accomplishments. But at that time the experts' word had to be accepted. Therefore school administrators who were convinced that the school had a responsibility toward the more severely intellectually handicapped children responded by emphasizing that the program they were instituting on this level was developed on a different basis—a strictly nonacademic curriculum, geared to socialization, learning of personal and social habits, and other so-called "life skills."

Due largely to the growing influence and responsible leadership from the Associations for Retarded Children, and due also to the success of many of the classes and schools sponsored by these associations in at least proving that many moderately and severely retarded children could spend 4 hours in orderly behavior in a classroom, more and more public school programs were initiated, in spite of the opposition. However, disturbing findings soon began to appear in educational and psychological journals. A large number of these studies indicated that the children in the classes of the trainable level were not showing any appreciable progress and did not seem to compare favorably with children of equal intellectual handicap who had not been in school. There is neither time nor much justification to report more in detail on these studies which, of course, moved the opponents to say that their predictions had come true: Severely retarded children were incapable of learning.

However, in the early 1960s there appeared a study which put a totally different perspective on this controversy. Dr. L. F. Cain and Dr. S. Levine of the San Francisco State College came to the conclusion that there had been a basic weakness in the many studies on the effectiveness of classes on the trainable level. Namely, the focus had been on the learning of the children and not on the teaching by the teachers. Therefore, in their study entitled *Effects of Community and Institutional School Programs on Trainable Mentally Retarded Children* (Cain & Levine, 1963), the spotlight was on *what* was being taught, and under what circumstances. Their procedure was as ingenious as it was simple. They secured the cooperation of school administrators and teachers and developed schedules for measuring classroom activities against the stated objectives of the program. Skilled observers then attended the classes and carefully analyzed minute by minute what took place. The results were most revealing: More than half of the time the children were in school was categorized as noninstructional; only one quarter was devoted to instruction related to the basic purpose of the program. In other words, expressing these findings in a simple efficiency rating, the programs observed in different schools in different communities as well as in a residential institution showed an efficiency rating of 9% to 11%.

Obviously, no school program could or should ever operate on a 100% efficiency rating; we are not dealing with machines. But the findings of the Cain and Levine study (1963) pointed up a glaring weakness in the teaching procedures. Certainly the children could not be expected to learn if the teachers did not know how to teach. Permit me to add here parenthetically that in our consultation visits too, to other countries, my wife and I have frequently encountered evidence of the same problem—a most distressing amount of time being wasted in such classes on inconsequential activities or just plain inactivity.

In the brief time available here, I cannot possibly do justice to the specific findings of this aspect of the study.

Those of you concerned with teacher training will find the specific examples of "high-adequate" and "low-adequate" teaching exceedingly useful. What I want to underline in this context, because it is applicable in many other countries, is that the overall weakness in the program of these classes was the low expectancy the teachers had of the capacity of their children.

In other words, as I pointed out earlier, the emphasis had been so much on the incapacity of the children, on all the things they could *not* do, that there was a general failure to hold up the children to standards of performance. Furthermore, the study concluded that the program had been devised on an assumption that these children have a low energy level and diminished vitality, and for that reason, too, few demands should be made on them. Finally, the many categorical statements made about "trainable" children apparently resulted in an inadequate realization by the teachers, in the day-to-day classroom activities, of the wide range of abilities the children actually presented, and as a result there was insufficient individual attention, encouragement, and insistence.

In fairness to the authors of this excellent study, I need to say here that the scope of their work went much beyond what I have emphasized in our context and included, among other things, a social competence scale in the evaluation of the children's progress or lack of progress, which was a major contribution and is becoming internationally recognized. However, my reason for dealing at length with this study is that it signaled the beginning of a more realistic attitude toward the teaching of moderately and severely retarded children in the United States. Of course, there were other significant studies that have contributed to a reorientation of teaching on this level, such as those dealing with frustration as a necessary factor in the learning process.

Circuitous thinking has been at the root of our educational problem: Because of prevailing beliefs, retarded children are treated in certain ways that intensify their weakness, and as a result they perform more inadequately, a result that is taken as inherent in their defect instead of as related to their experiential background. Thus preconceptions about the needs and potentials of the retarded result in specific ways of handling them which in turn result in a lower performance level. Once we free ourselves from these traditional preconceptions (which you can find plentifully represented even in recently published psychological textbooks), we can concentrate on minimizing, overcoming, or indeed preventing the development of many of these performance limitations.

All of this is finding expression in new thinking about the training of teachers for these classes. As long as it was felt that these children as a group had a very low learning potential, recommendations were made repeatedly that the more severe the mental handicap of the children, the less extensive need be the teacher's training, and some leading educators indeed recommended that teacher training as such was not necessary for classes on the trainable level. Today it is recognized that a high degree of teaching skill and formal training is required to do justice to that task, and the federal government now makes available substantial sums to strengthen university-level teacher training programs in special education including those concerned with moderately and severely retarded children.

In summary, very considerable progress has been made during the past 10 years, but there remain several problem areas. One relates to the fact that classes on a trainable level have in general been kept in isolation, that is to say, in separate buildings. A significant finding of the Cain and Levine study (1963) was that this kept the teachers away from the mainstream of educational thinking and deprived them of the stimulation that would come from relationships with teachers of other types of children.

There is much recognition that classroom space and classroom equipment require special attention. The need to provide differential programs for different age and ability groups implies that only in very large cities can these classes be expected to be within a reasonable distance of the children's homes. Transportation, always a major problem, will thus become more difficult, while in less populated areas children will need to be accommodated overnight during the school week, a program that is only in its earliest beginnings.

When classes on a trainable level were first started, many administrators felt that children should not be admitted until age 8 or 9. In contrast, today there is wide agreement that a preschool experience is very essential. I was interested to hear that the 4-year-old granddaughter of Vice-President Humphrey, a child with Down syndrome (mongolism), is already attending a preschool class.

One final comment on the subject of schooling. I am well aware that I have underplayed the technical aspects of instruction and, instead, dwelt to a considerable extent on the "behind the scenes" (or should I say "behind the classroom"?) struggle between opposing views regarding severe intellectual handicap. I have done so because without understanding these philosophical controversies it is hard to appreciate the obstacles we have encountered in the United States in the development of rational, effective school programs for these children....

CHAPTER 4
WHOM DO WE CALL MENTALLY RETARDED?

From "Whom Do We Call Retarded?" New Neighbors (chap. 3), 1974, Washington, DC: President's Committee on Mental Retardation, reprinted with permission

This book is about people, people referred to as being mentally retarded. Through the centuries much has been said about people referred to as mentally retarded, about their being dangerous, evil, possessed, or, to the contrary, special gifts from heaven, "holy innocents."

Many of these beliefs live on. One can encounter them even today almost anywhere in the United States as plans are discussed for community residences for mentally retarded persons.

Yet mentally retarded individuals have lived in our communities since time immemorial. Over the past decades many of them have gone to public schools, not by the thousands, but by the millions; in increasing numbers they are employed in business, industry, and government. They travel by bus and subway, go to ball games and movies, and some even vote at the polls.

This is not an idealized picture, but it is just not a complete picture. Many mentally retarded individuals, severely and multiply handicapped, whose functions and activities are extremely curtailed, spend their days in idleness in institutions.

First, then, we must learn that being called mentally retarded has very little meaning. Mental retardation is not a very descriptive or revealing term; it cannot convey an adequate picture. There is too wide a difference between the retarded young adult who leaves his community residence in the morning, joining the subway crowd on his way to work, and another retarded person who spends his day in the ward of one of our large state institutions, idly shuffling about.

In the face of such a wide range within the group considered to be mentally retarded, efforts have been made through the years to establish a terminology for the different degrees of this handicap. In the early part of this century, people differentiated between idiots, imbeciles, and morons, depending on the extent of their mental retardation, with the moron being the least severely involved.

With the introduction of the intelligence test, developed by Binet in France and brought to this country by Goddard, it became an accepted practice to relate these three terms to specific IQ scores[1]: *idiot* for those scoring below 25, *imbecile* 25 to 50, and *moron* 50 to 70 or 75. Later on the terms *severe*, *moderate*, and *mild* replaced those terms, but conceptually no change occurred. It was firmly believed that not only could the degree of mental retardation be definitively tied to fairly restricted scores on intelligence tests but, more important

---

[1] The concept of the intelligence quotient (IQ) as related to Binet's mental age was developed by W. Stern.

yet, that this was an unchanging static designation. Not only "once retarded, always retarded," but also "once moderately retarded, always moderately retarded." The IQ, it was commonly accepted, was fixed. Moreover, it was believed that the IQ ratings and the three-part classification—mild, moderate, severe—could be tied very closely to a level of functioning, circumscribing quite narrowly what such a person could not do in terms of daily living and learning. Whether a person received an IQ of 71 or 68, of 52 or 49, could have the most far-reaching consequences for his lifetime, because that difference was the key to decisions about the service which he would receive or from which he "had to be" excluded, and more likely it was the latter. As one educator [Albert T. Murphy] has succinctly expressed it, "While the difference between *becoming* or not becoming mentally subnormal may often be slight, the difference between being and not being mentally subnormal may be considerable" (as quoted in Blatt & Kaplan, 1966).

Overall, the steady progress of urbanization, industrialization, and specialization and the sharply increasing life tempo and competitiveness decreased the tolerance for retarded individuals, and less and less was there a place for them in the community, socially or even physically.

In the late 1940s and early 50s, into this situation broke the movement or, more appropriately, the rebellion of parents of mentally retarded children. Throughout the United States and Canada, in England, France, and Scandinavian countries, in Australia and New Zealand, these parents stood up and demanded that their children not be denied the privilege of schooling, vocational training, and meaningful occupations.

Although some educators quickly supported the parents' demands (and, indeed, a few school systems had heretofore for many years successfully conducted classes, not just for mildly but also for moderately retarded children), overall the field of education reacted negatively. The education profession remembered that high hopes for the educability of mentally retarded individuals during the second half of the 19th century had led to severe disillusionment, and to this was added the negative impetus of the "eugenic scare" during the first two decades of the 20th century, which looked upon the mentally retarded person as a menace to the well-being of society.

When parents pushed on and in many communities actually organized classes for the moderately retarded (that is, children with an IQ between 50 and 25), educators responded with a terminological sleight-of-hand, the effect of which is still haunting community planning. They introduced a supposed philosophical and methodological difference between educability and trainability. Mildly retarded children, those with an IQ above 50, were termed educable; the moderately retarded were considered ineducable but trainable. Also, many prominent leaders in special education believed that this "training" was not a responsibility of the public schools but a "welfare" job. Those below the "trainable" level, the educators chose to call "custodial" cases, suggesting that nothing more than safekeeping could meet their needs.

In the ensuing years, this viewpoint failed to prevail as, under pressure from parents, legislation was enacted in more and more states making the education of the so-called trainable child a mandated task of the public schools. However, the terminology remained, and with it the static viewpoint toward mental retardation on which it was founded.

This terminological effort of the special educators created serious and pervasive damage in two ways. Without sufficient evidence a sharp dichotomy was created between the learning process and learning capacity along the hairline of an IQ of 50. Furthermore, what might have been justifiable as a designation of two different teaching methods was perverted into a label affixed to individual children with the clear implication that a child, once designated trainable, could hardly be expected to move up to the more advanced type of instruction appropriate for educability. Unfortunately, the labeling did not stop here, but postschool community services such as vocational training centers and workshops adopted it as well, thereby carrying over the label of ineducability into adulthood, though the tasks to be performed by mentally retarded adults in a work situation might differ sharply from those in a classroom situation. Fortunately, the rather negative exclusion-oriented attitude of professional educators changed radically, most noticeably following the mid-60s. This shift in attitude culminated in a strong policy statement passed at the 1971 annual conference of the Council of Exceptional Children, the national organization of teachers, supervisors, and administrators in special education. This significant six-page document entitled "Basic Commitments and Responsibilities to Exceptional Children" explicitly states that education is the right of all children and that educational opportunities should not be denied to any child regardless of his potential for contributing to society.

While the foregoing developments took place in the field of special education, other changes occurred in the general terminology and classification of mental retardation. The American Association on Mental Deficiency (AAMD), in 1959, issued a revision of its *Manual on Terminology and Classification* (Heber) which contained three important changes. In contrast to other classification schemes, such as that in use by psychiatrists which tended to lump together all retarded persons with an IQ below 50 as essentially incapable of development and in need only of protective care, the 1959 AAMD classification, on the basis of demonstrated differential capacity and performance, suggested a three-level division of those with IQ below 50 into moderately, severely, and profoundly retarded. Furthermore, in the definition of mental retardation, this revision added to the factor "subaverage intellectual functioning" a second factor relating to social adaptation, "impairment in adaptive behavior." Finally, the *Manual* brought into the realm of mental retardation a grouping formerly known as having borderline intelligence. It did so by decreeing that (subject to the criterion of impairment in adaptive behavior) a differing mathematical cut-off point was to delineate mental retardation (to wit: one standard deviation below the norm) and that this psychometric grouping of people would henceforth be designated as borderline mentally retarded.

The first change, the creation of the new category of profound mental retardation, proved to be very useful from a practical viewpoint; it focused attention on this long-neglected group of individuals who populated the back wards of the state institutions. Studies and demonstration projects soon revealed that this group could respond far better to simple training efforts than had been assumed, and was even more responsive to environmental change when the back wards were changed into something a little bit more resembling human habitation. Furthermore, in many cases the severe physical impairments with which these individuals were afflicted appeared to be a major factor in their extremely low level of performance, and upon remediation (e.g., through orthopedic surgery, physical therapy, and so forth) a distinct improvement in their level of functioning occurred. This suggested that the group might be better referred to as profoundly handicapped rather than as profoundly mentally retarded.

There was a great deal of positive response from the field to the second recommended change, the addition of the concept of adaptive behavior. Unfortunately, however, tests for the application of this new criterion were still in the early stages of development and 15 years later are still not part of most psychological evaluations. In other words, in spite of increasing doubt about the sufficiency of the intelligence test in the determination of mental retardation, it has remained from a practical viewpoint the sole determinant.

Yet more significant…was the response to the third recommendation, the establishment of the new "borderline" category within mental retardation, which vastly increased the supposed number of retarded individuals in the United States. What happened was that 14 years later, in 1973, the American Association on Mental Deficiency published yet another revision of its *Manual* (Grossman, 1973) and with one turn of the printing press removed from millions of American citizens the burden imposed on them in 1959 of being presumed to be mentally retarded, albeit on the borderline level only. AAMD simply lowered the upper cut-off point for mental retardation not one but two standard deviations (e.g., an IQ of 68 on the Stanford Binet test), subject of course to the second criterion, impairment of adaptive behavior.

Here, then, this chapter's question "Whom do we call mentally retarded?" comes into sharp focus and brings forth a rather disturbing answer. We call mentally retarded those whom "we" choose to call so. And, who is the "we"? In this case of classification and terminology, it was a professional organization working in the field of mental retardation which entrusted this task to a committee and did not even see a need to have the sweeping revisions ratified by a vote of the membership. Thus, in an unmistakable way the American Association on Mental Deficiency has clearly supported the thesis put forth by one outstanding social scientist active in the field of mental retardation, Dr. Jane Mercer of the University of California. Dr. Mercer maintains that mental retardation is not so much a clinical designation based on compelling evidence as it is a social status conferred on individuals by whatever societal group has been given, or has taken upon itself, the right to so label people.

The President's Committee on Mental Retardation has illustrated this view with its widely distributed booklet *The Six-Hour Retarded Child* (1970), the child who 5 days a week, from nine to three, has the status in school of being retarded but who is not considered so while moving about in the community.

But this is not the only example. Those concerned with statistical studies in mental retardation have long been aware of an intriguing phenomenon: The number of "known" mentally retarded persons in any community drops sharply for the older out-of-school group. Once a young adult has left school and on his own has secured employment in the community, he may "lose" his status as a retarded individual and may be accepted at his place of employment, as well as in the community at large, as just another young citizen.

In other words, as we set out to develop new plans for community services for mentally retarded persons, we need to remember that tens of thousands of substantially mentally retarded children, adolescents, and adults are now and have been for many years living, walking, and working in our cities and towns, have attended public schools, have gone to camp, have used streetcars and subways, have voted and held a vast variety of jobs. While many of them, maybe the majority, were and are known to some as retarded individuals, many are not so recognized in day-to-day living. Yet other individuals are so handicapped or conduct themselves in such a fashion as to be seen as manifestly retarded. We must understand that the *status of being retarded is open to change*, and the record will show that our predictive capability is limited.

Less dramatic perhaps, but to the individual involved of greater significance, is a further and related phenomenon: The level or degree of mental retardation originally bestowed upon an individual by a clinic, school, or institution may also change. The individual who once sat in an institutional back ward, half naked, aimlessly rocking back and forth, and "obviously" profoundly retarded, may later be seen in a sheltered workshop in the community, operating some simple mechanical equipment, properly dressed, and maintaining human contacts—verbal or nonverbal—with others around him.

Of course, at least presently, certain groups of children or adults need more or less extensive nursing care for an unspecifiable time. But their condition clearly does not require confinement in a large state institution. They have a right and the capacity to be in an appropriate community facility, with an open door leading to a less restrictive, less restraining environment. Only time will tell who will use that open door.

And that brings us to the question: How many retarded persons are there in our community? This invokes a counterquestion: How retarded is retarded? Shall we be guided by the 1959 or 1973 definition of the American Association on Mental Deficiency? The by now traditional statistical view was predicted on a 3% figure. But no one has yet been able to find the 3% mentally retarded persons in any large unselected population group. Two scholars who have given this question much study, Professors Burton Blatt and George Tarjan, put the incidence of mental retardation in the general population at no more than 1%, and quite likely less.

Furthermore, even if one could say with certainty that a given community has today 100 individuals waiting for a place in a community group home or other facility, it would be hard, indeed impossible, to predict for how long each one of them would need to stay there or how soon they could move to "regular" unsupervised living quarters. Broad statistical generalizations will be of very limited use in this context.

Our knowledge of the developmental potential of individuals labeled retarded is as yet insufficient for long-range estimates. A parallel will make this clear: Had we rushed in, nationwide, in the 1950s and 60s to build special schoolhouses for children considered to be only "trainable," we would now have white elephants on our hands from coast to coast.

The question "Whom do we call retarded?" is best responded to by a counterquestion: Why *call* anyone retarded? Webster's dictionary says "to call" means among other things "to utter in a loud or distinct voice," "to regard or characterize as to a certain kind."

Perhaps the significance of the question and counterquestion will become more apparent if we take our cue from the last definition and explore what "certain kind" we mean when we use the term *mental retardation*.

At least to some extent the answer to this question will surely come from young and not so young mentally retarded adults themselves, whose emergence from the once-nebulous mass characterized as mentally retarded is providing us with an exciting and challenging drama. One can already clearly discern the first indications that some of these people, once known as "docile retardates," are no longer willing to sit in the back of the bus. Education is a powerful tool; the withholding of education and of knowledge has been practiced through the ages of benevolent as well as oppressive rulers in church and state. Education and a new tool, "advocacy," are now helping the retarded citizen to assert himself and to protest a label that he sees as a libel.

Part 2

Human Potential, Human Rights

Editors' Introduction to Part 2

Although current practice involves individuals with disabilities in the design and implementation of services, professionals continue to write about what they can do "for" people with retardation rather than what they can do together. The undesirable "we-them" structure of the provider-recipient relationship remains dominant. What began as a notion that "the person with retardation is not so bad" has become more positive over time; that person is more capable, more able to make decisions, more able to be included in society's mainstream. But that person is still in need of us, the professionals, to make the most of his or her life.

When Dr. Dybwad was completing his years at the National Association for Retarded Children, he had a chance to become more appreciative of the people who were called "retarded." His growing conviction that professionals had been far too negative in their past writing and had placed too much emphasis on what people with retardation didn't know was confirmed as he met more people labeled "retarded." His international travels provided opportunities for Dr. Dybwad to see how independently individuals with mental retardation could live and how well they could manage. It confirmed his sense of the contrast between his experiences and common practices in the field. Programs of intelligence testing, for example, however benevolent in their conception, led in practice to greater emphasis on weaknesses and bolstered a "deficit model" of service provision.

These speeches present one of Dr. Dybwad's major contributions to the field of disability: the notion that a model that is based on *strengths* supports growth, inclusion, capacity, and choice. He believes that as long as professionals continue to simply invite people with disabilities only to advise the "knowing" professionals, the "we-they" dichotomy will remain strong.

Chapter 5
Rights and Duties

Excerpt from a presentation, "The Mentally Retarded in the Changing Society,"
at the Third Asian Conference on Mental Retardation, Bangalore, India, November 1977

There has been much international discussion in the most recent years regarding the rights of handicapped people, particularly after the United Nations adopted in December 1971 the Declaration of the Rights of Mentally Retarded Persons, and 4 years later, in December 1975, the Declaration of the Rights of Disabled Persons.... While reviewing the proceedings of the First Asian Conference on Mental Retardation in Manila, I came across the following statement:

> Whereas the West seems preoccupied with the assertion of "rights" as our hope—for example, the Declaration of the Rights of the Child in the United Nations—the Orient seems more inclined to the Vedic principles of duties or what might be called compassionate values and hopes. These Vedic biases have pervaded most Asian cultures, even those which were superceded by Muslimism. In these cultures, the concept of "rights" is exotic, apart from the fact that rights logically presuppose duties.

Eager to understand this statement more adequately, I consulted an Indian colleague, who is professionally engaged in mental retardation in the town where I work but who periodically returns to India with her husband. As we talked about this, we did not see here so much a contradiction between East and West, because in the West, too, the religious viewpoint and the traditional cultural pattern do indeed speak more of duties, of love for one's fellowman, of charity as a religious obligation. We concluded that discussions of rights (as against duties) make their appearance with the advent of industrialization, the loosening of family ties, and increasing mobility, all of which tend to deprive many persons of security and protection previously assured by the extended family and the neighborhood.

The morning following my conversation with this Indian colleague, by strange coincidence, a letter arrived from a rehabilitation facility in India, asking me to bring along some materials about the legal rights of the handicapped, as they were eager to have more information on that aspect of the work. When I discussed this with my wife, Dr. Rosemary Dybwad, she produced from her resource files the April 1968 issue of the *Indian Journal of Social Work*, which on 90 pages reported on the 14th National Conference of the Indian Council on Social Welfare, held in Madras in December 1967, wholly devoted to discussion of human rights and the realities of social welfare....

It seems to me to be of great significance that this discussion took place in India 10 months before the International League of Societies for the Mentally Handicapped promulgated in Jerusalem its Declaration of General and Special Rights of the Mentally Retarded, adopted by the United Nations 3 years later.

But then, lo and behold, 2 days later my Indian colleague produced from her own professional library a volume entitled *The Social Work Forum, 1947-1957*, being a selective rendering of social work thought as reflected in the deliberations of the annual sessions of the Indian Conference of Social Work. And thus I discovered that already 30 years ago, in 1947, the Indian Conference on Social Work included in its recommendations a Bill of Rights, albeit for the physically handicapped, and, furthermore, recommended "that special schools with professionally trained staff be provided for the care, education, guidance and training of the physically *and* mentally handicapped children."

As I contemplated the surprising discovery of this early and very intensive discussion by Indian social workers on individual rights, my mind flashed back to the days in the early 1960s when my wife and I were codirectors of a mental retardation project for the International Union for Child Welfare. In the Geneva headquarters of the Union, there hung on the walls a most interesting collection of documents, namely copies of the Declaration of the Rights of the Child, also known as the Geneva Declaration, translated into the major languages of the world and signed either by former heads of state or by national leaders....

The world-wide depression years, the demise of the League of Nations, and World War II pushed this Declaration into the background, but following the war the United Nations promulgated in 1948 the Universal Declaration of Human Rights, and in 1959 it adopted, under the title Declaration of the Rights of the Child, an enlarged version of the original Geneva Declaration which had been signed by Mahatma Gandhi and other leaders of Asian countries.

My purpose in reciting to you these facts is to underline for you that the U.N. Declaration on the Rights of Mentally Retarded Persons and the subsequent U.N. Declaration on the Rights of Disabled Persons were not just the project of some advanced theoretical position in the field of rehabilitation, as is believed by some of my more conservative colleagues in various countries, including my own. Rather, these declarations grew out of an international consciousness of human rights that had as one of its identifiable sources the Geneva Declaration promulgated 54 years ago, and already then supported by leaders in Asian countries....

As is the case with the so frequently misunderstood term *normalization*, the specific implementation of the assurance of handicapped persons' rights must, of course, be done in a manner that is appropriate to the country where action is taken. In other words, how a specific right is identified and implemented may vary widely from country to country. Laws are not absolute but are culture-bound and at various times may be differently interpreted.

Thus, one of the reports of that 1968 Social Welfare convention in Madras stated:

> We have thought too long on the Western type of relief. We need to blaze a new trail of evolving indigenous methods, techniques and institutions, and also welfare measures which can respond to the voluminous needs of a developing society under conditions obtaining therein.

The relevance of this rather lengthy discussion rests with a development which, to a greater or lesser extent, is observable in all countries. Mental retardation is no longer a predominantly child-centered problem. Belatedly there has been recognition that mentally retarded children grow up to be mentally retarded adults, and that their life span as adults by far exceeds their life span as children. The rights of a child are presumed to be taken care of by his parents. The problem to which we must now devote our attention is how we can make sure that the mentally retarded adult can be reasonably assured of his rights. And since we agree that rights are the other side of the coin of responsibilities, how can we make sure that in years to come the mentally retarded adult is given a reasonable chance to assume and learn to carry out those responsibilities of which he is capable? Here lies a challenge worthy of discussion during this Third Asian Conference on Mental Retardation.

CHAPTER 6
THE CONCEPT OF NORMALIZATION

*Excerpt from a presentation, "The Undeveloped Resource at the Edge of Change,"
at the Fall Conference on Mental Retardation, cosponsored by the California Council for Retarded Children
and the American Association on Mental Deficiency, San Francisco, November 1968*

Let me leave you with some thoughts of a little more general nature. I implied earlier that I certainly agreed with President Kennedy that there were some other countries in the world that, in this particular area, were far ahead of us; and as you know, the Scandinavian countries are countries where this is particularly the case. And from them has come to us a concept that only now we are beginning to really see more clearly. And I include myself most definitely in this "we," although, as you know, I have some rather close ties over there, and I have been visiting innumerable times in these countries, particularly in the area of mental retardation.

But only now I begin to see how terribly important is the concept to which they ascribe their entire mental retardation approach—the concept of normalization. It is a concept that is elegant in its simplicity and parsimony. It can be readily understood by everyone and, at the same time, it has far-reaching implications. When you visit mental retardation services in Denmark or Sweden and, observing some things, ask, "Why do you do this?" they most likely will just say, "This is the normal way of doing things." That is why they have this kind of room for the mentally retarded; that is why they have this kind of schedule; that is why they have that kind of arrangement. It is the normal thing! Proceeding from that assumption, they deny the normal situation—the normal arrangement, the normal furnishings, the normal food, the normal eating time, the normal bed time, the normal way of being addressed as a human being—only when there is some very compelling reason.

From my years of visiting institutions for the mentally retarded (although I started out at Letchworth Village 30 years ago, my intensive visiting goes back only 8 to 10 years), I would say we do the opposite: We simply take for granted the abnormal, and we extend the normal only as a privilege. Hence, this principle of normalization—this insistence on thinking of people in a normal way—is so very, very important, because it leads you to think more and more of people as human beings and to become more and more concerned about the harmful effect of categories and labeling and categorical labelings.

The other day I had to look up a letter I had written to Mr. Krause. Just to show you that I do not just shoot off my mouth loudly in public, but I very often quietly shoot it off in correspondence, let me read what I wrote to him in June 1967:

> I have just seen the May bulletin of the Sacramento Association for the Retarded which states on page 1 that at Sonoma State Hospital, with a population of 3,500, the number of non-ambulatory patients has soared from 400 to almost 1,200. I am very much concerned about that statement because it implies a real danger in terms of official treatment policy toward these individuals. What does it mean that a patient is

nonambulatory? Do you realize that both my children were nonambulatory, yet subsequently were able to go through college and even graduate school? As a matter of fact, I have heard that all children start out nonambulatory. How old are these 1,200 nonambulatory patients at Sonoma? What is their background? Why are they non-ambulatory? Is there a substantial number among them whose condition calls for orthopedic intervention? Is there a substantial number among them where ambulation will depend on intervention by intensive training programs? How many of them show an advanced degree of, e.g., hydrocephalus, which makes ambulation a physical improbability, if not impossibility?

I hope you see what I am trying to convey to you: This illustrates the concept of normalization. You just cannot call 1,200 people nonambulatory and then try to prescribe for them on that basis.

The broad concept of normalization can be implemented by some subsidiary principles, and I want very quickly to name them to you so you can see that we really have a frame of reference through which we can tackle our problems in a sensible and thoughtful basis.

The first principle by which the Scandinavians implement normalization is integration, which refers to those measures and practices which maximize a retarded person's community living and community participation. Of course there are degrees to this, very obviously. But the main point is that we should not be exclusive, but inclusive. Individualization as an essential feature of normalization assures social approval by granting maximum integration into those normal life patterns of which a retarded person is capable at any given time. This simply means a complete turning away from past practices. Let me give you an example. There is now in the State of Illinois a project on the drawing board—it has gone through preliminary approval—where they have for a group of severely and profoundly retarded individuals a plan with houses for eight. I did not say *units*; I said *houses* for eight, in order to have a grouping where one can do a maximum job of integration. There are other states trying to move in this direction. Let me not be tempted to tell more about this.

Dispersal is another principle the Scandinavian countries use. Of course you have started out on a very important aspect of this with the establishment of regional centers. And in that respect, may I say I am very happy that you have not committed one mistake which has cost progressive Connecticut headaches to no end. Connecticut has combined its regional centers with residential facilities and now the whole concept of the regional center and its basic function, which you have well defined here in your state is, in Connecticut, in extreme danger. This is so because the fellow who runs the residential facility for 200 human beings is so taken up with it, has to worry so much about important things like toilet paper—and I happen to believe that that is important—and soap and towels and proper toilet seats and all such things, that he has no time to develop the community facilities on which the center's activities should focus.

So I am very happy that in your beginning dispersal you have certainly moved in the right direction, and I want to echo what was said this morning that the thought of having the existing institutions serve as regional centers would scuttle the whole plan or, at least, pervert it totally. Your State Report, of course, foreshadowed dispersal when it said you needed to develop many kinds of community-related residential services.

The third of the Scandinavian principles is specialization. You can travel through a Scandinavian country and find a little place where you see these older institutions housing maybe 40 aged people who live by themselves. It is a specialized institution. In other words, not only have they dispersed institutions but dispersed institutions need to be specialized because they cannot possibly serve all comers as some of our privately operated institutions have been tempted to do, and found difficult to do. Specialization, then, goes along with dispersal and means that we are going to have specialized facilities, such as for the aged, emergency homes, school homes, hostels for the people who can work in the community. And may I just add that in Sweden they now actually have developed some hostels right in an apartment house. One additional comment: When it comes to small residential facilities, we should stop building and try to use, until we have gained more experience, existing community facilities, because the purposely built hostels all have a tendency to be like little institutions. Strangely, it appears to be a most difficult task to build an informal place.

The final principle in Scandinavia is one I think we have readily understood ever since the report of President Kennedy's Panel, and that is the question of continuity. Continuity is essential in terms of available services but so is continuity between those aspects of a person's life which are supported by special services and those which are not. There is a danger that we develop continuity in such a way that we slide a fellow along from service to service and so overprotect him that he never has a chance to try and see how he might do on his own, an opportunity he should have.

This quick summary of what we have learned from the Scandinavian countries will convey to you that we can really build into our frame of reference some basic principles in such a way that we can develop rational programs. If you will in community as much as in state planning make it your habit to refer to these principles and to check yourself that you really do apply them, you will have an orderly process in which to proceed planning and not just a process to "make do."

I talked with you today in great frankness and thought I could do so because I really feel that I am among friends in California and that my long relationship with the California Council and the continuing correspondence we have, which, by the way, never ceased even during the years I was over in Switzerland, gave me the freedom to talk with you straightforwardly.

Mental retardation is a problem in which we are faced in this country with a very sad situation—a situation which really is a disgrace to our country. But, at the same time, let me say that I have told the Swedes and the Danes that in a few years they are going to come to us to learn. In a few years, they will see that when we really apply ourselves and free ourselves of the shackles of the past, we will do things out of technical know-how and also out of our strength of conviction and our way of life that will make them jealous. I do not know the difference between an optimist and a pessimist; I just know I am an optimist, and I look at the tasks ahead of us from a very bright and sunny perspective. But at the same time, I must again say, you will never get where you need to go unless you first, very clearly, admit to yourselves where you are now and what needs to be done to move you forward.

Chapter 7
Ethical and Legal Problems in Rehabilitation and Medicine

*From "Ethical and Legal Problems in Rehabilitation and Medicine,"
The Changing Rehabilitation World: Into the 21st Century (pp. 10-15), 1986,
New York: United Cerebral Palsy of New York City, Inc., reprinted with permission*

As one tries to assess the impact of the changing rehabilitation world and tries to forecast its future in the 21st century, it is necessary to keep in mind the fact that—notwithstanding some early rather specialized beginnings—rehabilitation as a major area of human service really did not come into public awareness until the second half of the present century.

Without question it was as a result of greatly expanded rehabilitation work during and as a result of World War II that the field gained governmental support and developed a massive investment from various disciplines, with medicine in the lead. That this did not just occur in the United States but on a wide international scale is demonstrated by the famous Recommendation 99 passed by the General Conference of the International Labor Organization (ILO) in 1955, the Recommendation Concerning Vocational Rehabilitation of the Disabled, a comprehensive blueprint for rehabilitation action in the industrial countries of the world. That this blueprint included a section entitled Special Provisions for Disabled Children and Young Persons, urging the establishment of special education programs, underlines the progressive stance of this ILO document; after all it was not until 10 years later that UNESCO initiated steps to create a special Education Unit within its structure.

In our country medical, surgical, pharmaceutical advances, technological achievements in the development of prostheses and devices supporting activities of daily living, novel approaches to work training and placement, and, last but not least, programs of special education for children, have resulted in truly spectacular improvement in the lives of disabled persons previously deemed to be beyond effective intervention. In barely four decades tremendous progress has been made on a broad front of physical and mental disabilities, and as a result long-cherished beliefs—once perceived as definitive scientific facts—have been demolished, and basic assumptions of professional practice in a variety of disciplines are no longer tenable. Above all there has been the remarkable liberation of an ever-growing number of people with severe disabilities from a state of helplessness and dependency.

Infants With Birth Defects

Not surprisingly, that rapid pace created a lag in societal perception of this new phenomenon and this in turn affected the lag in legal and ethical perspectives concerning persons with disabilities. Conflict situations were inevitable, and in the field of medicine they came to public attention first in the treatment of infants with serious birth defects. Reference has been made in earlier presentations at this conference to the case at Johns Hopkins University brought to public attention by the Kennedy Foundation film in 1971, and to Baby Doe, whose life was terminated in Bloomington, Indiana, in 1982. Interestingly, the problem of the presence of Down syndrome in a newborn which characterized both these cases was brought to public attention at a much earlier date. In 1961 the Columbia Broadcasting System introduced with considerable advance publicity a new television series called "The Defenders" dealing with the legal exploits of a father-son attorney team. Files of the Museum of Broadcasting in New York City reveal that the subject of the show which introduced the series was the story of a doctor who terminated—soon after birth—the life of an infant born with Down syndrome, with the tacit approval of the father. The mother, still recovering from anesthesia, had not seen the baby. When the doctor's action becomes known, he is indicted on a charge of murder, but in a climactic courtroom scene the father-son lawyer team succeeds in getting the charge substantially reduced. Thus, 24 years ago a nationwide audience was introduced for the first time, it appears, to Down syndrome (then still called mongolism) as a reason for infanticide.

For my discussion of legal and ethical problems related to the termination of life of infants with disabilities, I shall use a case summary taken verbatim in its entirety from an article published in 1982 in *Connecticut Medicine*, the journal of the Connecticut Medical Association, written by Thayer Baldwin, a lawyer, then chief of Health System Regulation, Connecticut State Department of Health Services.

> Case #1. The low birth weight, full term infant was transferred from another hospital on oxygen support. Problems noted early on included physical signs of Down's Syndrome, heart defect (probably AV canal), and probable duodenal stenosis. (The heart condition was operable, but with a high mortality rate.) The infant was prepared for duodenal surgery, however, the parents chose not to perform surgery. The mother did not want the baby to suffer or to ruin the lives of their other children. The parents requested that the hospital not get in touch with a parent-support group as had been suggested by a social worker. A physician-supported, subsequent parent decision was made to discontinue all support. A statement signed by the parents appeared in the record which stated their decision against abdominal surgery and their decision to withdraw "medical support" and their understanding of the "full meaning of this decision."
>
> All "support" was discontinued on the fourth day of life, including oral feedings (which were not feasible) and intravenous nourishment. These activities were substantiated by doctors' orders and nurses' records. At death (at 23 days old) the infant showed a substantial weight loss from birth. (Baldwin, 1982)

Parents' Role in Decision Making

I have chosen this case because it establishes clearly that the attending physician had decided on and arranged for surgical intervention but canceled it at the parents' request. This not only raises a question about the physician's compliance with his professional and statutory obligation, but it also raises questions about the function of the hospital in this case. Incidentally, what about reimbursement to the hospital for 19 days during which neither nourishment nor any medical care was given? This situation can be put into sharper focus by asking the following: Since the decision to starve the child was made not by the medical staff but by the parents, and does not involve medical attention, should a parent who has adequate hospital insurance be allowed to take such an infant home for domestic starvation? I believe that this reduction *ad absurdum* highlights the legal quagmire produced by the handling of this case.

A further word is needed regarding the mother's role in this case. In 1981 the American Medical Association published *Current Opinions of the Judicial Council,* which included the following statement regarding assurance of quality of life for seriously deformed newborn children:

> In caring for defective infants, the advice and judgment of the physician should be readily available but the decision whether to treat a severely defective infant and exert maximal efforts to sustain life should be the choice of the parents. The parents should be told the options, expected benefits, risks, and limits of any proposed care; how the potential for human relationships is affected by the infant's condition and relevant information and answers to their questions. (American Medical Association, 1981)

In like manner, the previously cited report of the Connecticut Health Department propounds that "the ultimate decision for treatment rests with the parent" (Baldwin, 1982). This policy of the American Medical Association is in direct contrast to the finding Professor Robertson, then at the University of Wisconsin Law School, put forth in his 1975 article "Involuntary Euthanasia of Defective Newborns: A Legal Analysis," the first thorough treatise on this subject. He holds that under no circumstances can a parent claim the right to make decisions regarding life and death of a child, and he points out that "…under existing law parents, physicians and hospital staff commit several crimes in withholding care, and that on the whole, with few exceptions, criminal liability may be both desirable and morally compelled" (Robertson, 1975). Considering that the American Medical Association, in general, insists on the physician having the primary role in all matters relating to the practice of medicine, this policy of yielding to the parental decision is indeed puzzling.

So far I have dealt with procedural matters, with the question of who may or may not make decisions, and under what circumstances, regarding life and death of infants. I am now coming to substantive questions, to a consideration of specific decisions.

Decisions and Facts

In an article entitled "Spina Bifida: The State of the Art of Medical Management," Anthony Gallo (1984), professor of pediatric neurosurgery at the Oregon Health Sciences University, states that good ethics begin with good facts, and I would add that similarly good legal process can only evolve from good facts. Dr. Gallo proceeds to point out that while in four distinct areas in the treatment of spina bifida significant advances have been made in recent years, greatly enhancing a favorable outcome, in many cases decisions not to treat such children at the risk of their dying are still made on the basis of outdated information.

This problem is even more acute in regard to children with Down syndrome. To this day one can find references in reputable journals to criteria for decision making as to which neonates with Down syndrome should be eliminated, criteria which are plainly nonsensical. Most quoted and yet most ridiculous is the notion put forth by Joseph Fletcher, professor of ethics and theology, that such decisions should be based in part on the intelligence level. It is of course absurd to think of trying to determine the intellectual potential of a newborn baby in the hospital nursery, but Fletcher (1972) goes further yet trying to delimit humanhood by suggesting that an IQ under 20 would characterize a "non-person," an IQ under 40, a "semi-person," with the obvious consequence that the "non-person" would be denied both constitutional and legal protection and could thus be eliminated with impunity. A report from the American Bar Association's Commission on the Mentally Disabled has this terse comment: "While philosophers and theologians have on occasion attempted to define critical indicia of 'humanhood' the argument is difficult to consider seriously in a legal context" (Sales et al., 1982).

In a similar vein, a group of physicians at the Oklahoma Health Science Center (Gross et al., 1983) in trying to give an aura of scientific objectivity to their process of selecting certain infants with spina bifida for nontreatment with the inherent risk of termination of life, is utilizing routinely a quality of life formula first developed by Anthony Shaw (1977), professor of surgery and pediatrics at the University of Virginia. The formula reads $QL = NE \times (H+S)$. Quality of life equals NE (the child's natural endowment, physical and intellectual) multiplied by H (the contribution the child can expect from his home and family) plus S (the probable contribution to the handicapped child from society). And all of this in the first weeks of an infant's life! Obviously such a formula could not withstand a 3-minute cross-examination by a second-year law student.

Considering Potential

Let us look at a specific case I have followed for a number of years, an individual with spina bifida who as a young child was rescued from the back wards of a large mental retardation state institution by a couple who subsequently adopted him. His medical problems have required repeated surgery but, although wheelchair bound, he has graduated from high school and is now attending a university in another city, living independently and driving a specially equipped motor car.

Clearly, the persons who placed him in the institution and those who kept him on a ward with low functioning children could have had no idea of that child's natural endowment and the probable contributions to him from society. Nor could anyone else have even vaguely guessed what would actually transpire up to the time of his enrollment in a university.

A word of explanation is needed here: I have made no reference to the Child Abuse Amendments of 1984, Public Law 98-157, the so-called Baby Doe Legislation, nor to the Federal Regulations and Guidelines to implement this 1984 legislation which were issued on April 15 of this year. Whether and to what extent this new legislation will affect the kind of medical practices I have discussed this morning any more than general legislation which has been on the books in the past remains to be seen. Infant Care Review Committees which are purely "in-house," which do not include appropriate, independent representatives from the community at large (call them advocates if you please), may all too easily becloud and complicate the situation by adding to the individual acts of a physician the defensive stance of the hospital. Such committees may serve well in institutions with good practices, but will serve poorly where they are most needed.

My second topic might be called "Beyond Baby Doe Into Later Life" and brings us more specifically into the context of rehabilitation. In a recent publication entitled *Everybody's Ethics: What Future for Handicapped Children?* written by Ann Shearer (1984a) and published by the Campaign for Mentally Handicapped People, an outstanding British advocacy group, the author points out that whatever eventual decision we reach about allowing severely handicapped infants to live or die will bring its own message about how we gauge the worth of people with disabilities in general.

The Phillip Becker Case

Consider the following situation: The parents of a 7-year-old boy are informed by the physician that their son urgently needs corrective heart surgery to avoid a debilitating condition which will lead to discomfort, pain, and eventually premature death. The parents refuse permission for surgery. Five years later, in 1978, their persistence in such refusal comes to public attention and the district attorney filed neglect proceedings. In court the parents pointed out that their son was born with Down syndrome, was therefore placed at birth in an institution, that his life was of little value and that he would be better off dead than alive. Strangely the court saw no reason to supersede the parents' wishes and denied the state's petition, thus in essence condemning the child to a premature death because his parents did not want him to live (Annas, 1979). The case was appealed to a superior court, which upheld what was essentially the verdict against the child (not the State) and successively both the State Supreme Court and the U.S. Supreme Court refused to act on further appeals. This of course was the well-known case of Phillip Becker, who as neonate was spared the fate of Baby Doe, but instead was subjected from birth to extreme deprivation in inappropriate institutional surroundings. The court reasoned, and the U.S. Supreme Court saw no reason to disagree, that since this 12-year-old boy had Down syndrome, the family's refusal to permit needed surgery took priority, even though Phillip had never been allowed to live as a part of that family.

Fortunately, in a subsequent action before another court (Herr, 1984), guardianship was awarded to a couple who had long befriended the boy. Today Phillip Becker is an outgoing, physically active adolescent, the surgery having been successfully carried out, and he has at least won his right to live, the U.S. Supreme Court to the contrary notwithstanding.

Neither the court that upheld the parents' refusal of medical care for Phillip Becker nor the court that later rescued him by granting guardianship took exception to the institutionalization of the boy from earliest infancy, which might easily have resulted in life-long confinement. In considering this matter I am reminded of the mother of a child with Down syndrome, and an activist in advocacy, who was asked by a reporter whether she was not in fact supporting the right-to-life movement. She said no, there was a difference, because she supported the right-to-live movement (*USA Today*, 1985).

The Justin Clark Case

Let me cite a case which is an interesting parallel to the situation of Phillip Becker because here the court denied guardianship as a means of continued institutionalizing of a person with cerebral palsy. Justin Clark was admitted to a large mental retardation institution in Canada when he was 2 years old, and the stifling institutional surroundings provided only minimal educational opportunities. His parents did not visit him or bring him home for visits. It is fair to say that in this retarding environment he functioned on a retarded level until he was finally given an opportunity, at the age of 12, to learn to use a communications board attached to his wheelchair. When he turned 18 the staff, responding to his pleas, found him eligible for community placement. When the father was informed about his plan, he disapproved and went to court seeking guardianship so he could legally veto any community placement. In the ensuing court hearing the judge rejected the testimony of physicians who appeared in support of the father's position because they had only general observations about the severity of Justin's disability, having nothing to say about the young man's actual functioning; in contrast, the judge was impressed with the way in which Justin was able to express himself about his future plans and said, "a courageous man, such as Justin Clark, is entitled to take a risk." The father's petition for guardianship was rejected.[1]

I selected this Canadian case because I hope that its happy outcome will motivate you to see how many persons with cerebral palsy are unjustly and inappropriately confined in institutions in your own state because of insufficient interplay between those charged with medical and legal protection respectively. It is safe to say that there are many hundreds of them in our country, and I know of cases where such individuals have tried for 5 years and more to gain their freedom from an inappropriate and loathsome institutionalization.

Freedom for severely disabled persons does not just mean absence of institutionalization. Their freedom can be severely curtailed when they are denied equipment or access to needed services. We must never forget that it was in the wealthy and progressive state of California that Ed Roberts, one of our great leaders in rehabilitation, as a young man was refused by the state rehabilitation agency a needed wheelchair and access to graduate education because a clinical evaluation judged him to be "not rehabilitable" (Bernstein, 1985). Since those days we have of course in the Rehabilitation Act of 1973 a law which specifically commands that priority be given to those with the most severe disabilities. Yet we have a long way to go in developing effective mechanisms on the state level so that the disabled person will indeed receive what the law provides.

One promising new avenue for the person with disability is the process of self-advocacy which is gaining strength under the impetus of the disability rights movement, and increasingly limits the dependency on bureaucratic agencies (Roberts, 1982). It also will result in a better chance for the individual to interact with the medical establishment and its power to give or withhold, to encourage or to stifle. Furthermore, by no means does the rise of self-advocacy diminish the effective voice of the parent movement whose pioneering in the 1950s and struggle in the 1960s have paved the way for today's recognition of disability rights.

The 20th century has given us so far great progress in rehabilitation and medicine—let us be sure that in the remaining 15 years we will resist successfully any trend of cutting back services and support, and will succeed in protecting and developing the legal bases for effective rehabilitation.

---

[1] 40 Ontario Reports (2nd) 383.

Chapter 8
Basic Legal Aspects in Providing Medical, Educational, Social, and Vocational Help to the Mentally Retarded

From "Basic Legal Aspects in Providing Medical, Educational, Social, and Vocational Help to the Mentally Retarded, 1973, The Journal of Special Education, 7 (1), 39-50, *copyright 1973 by PRO-ED, Inc., reprinted with permission*

Of the many accomplishments of the International League of Societies for the Mentally Handicapped in its first decade, none had a greater signature and more far-reaching effect than its 1967 Symposium on Legislative Aspects of Mental Retardation, which brought to Stockholm 30 representatives of 14 national member societies of the League. The Symposium clearly recognized the wide variations in legal administrative practices from country to country, based on resources as well as cultural and political traditions. The participants, nevertheless, found it possible to develop common agreement on standards that could guide the various countries in reviewing and changing legislative provisions for the mentally retarded.

Traditionally, this type of legislation had addressed itself mainly to the problem of constricting the mentally retarded, limiting their freedom of action, safeguarding their property, prescribing confinement in institutions, permitting their exclusion from vital services such as public schools, and imposing obligations on the parents or providing parent surrogates. The recommendations of the Stockholm Symposium reversed this negative approach and, instead, set forth some broad general principles encompassing the individual rights of the mentally retarded person as a human being. As the Conclusions of the Stockholm Symposium (International League, 1967) were distributed worldwide, the special section on individual rights was soon recognized as its key provision. A year later, at the Fourth Congress of the International League in Jerusalem, the delegates reformulated these conclusions into a Declaration of General and Special Rights of the Mentally Retarded.

A declaration of rights of the mentally retarded? Is that not going too far? Does this not imply that the International League lacked both a sense of reality and an understanding of political factors? Those who thought so—among them were prominent leaders in the movement of parents and friends for retarded children—were taken by surprise when they learned that, at the initiative of the government of France, this Declaration had been submitted to the United Nations Social Development Commission for consideration. But even the most optimistic observers were surprised when the Commission, without a negative vote, passed on the report with a favorable recommendation to the United Nations Economic and Social Council (ECOSOC). ECOSOC, in turn, reviewed the Declaration favorably and passed it on to the United Nations General Assembly with a recommendation for adoption. Among the few editorial changes, one added word illustrates how well the ECOSOC statesmen understood the problem: They amended "Rights of the Mental Retarded" to "Rights of Mentally Retarded Persons."[1]

What produced this remarkable turn of events? Is there any rational explanation for it? International developments in the field of human services provide an historical perspective for the Declaration on the Rights of the Mentally Retarded Persons. It was almost half a century ago, in 1923, when a leader in the Save the Children movement, Miss Eglantyne Jebb, spent an afternoon on Le Salève, the mountain overlooking Geneva, and wrote down her thoughts on the rights of children. This brief seven-point statement, which came to be known as the Geneva Declaration, was so forceful in its simplicity, so persuasive in pleading for the child as a person, that governments throughout the world became signatories to it. In the headquarters of the International Union for Child Welfare[2] in Geneva, there is an impressive display of the original document bearing the signatures of kings and queens and other heads of state.

Subsequently, in 1924, the Fifth Assembly of the League of Nations unanimously adopted the Geneva Declaration, and later that year the Fourth Pan-American Congress on Child Welfare did likewise. Unfortunately, however, World War II and the preceding years of international turmoil interrupted any further work along these lines. Nonetheless, for those working in the field of child welfare, Article 4 of the Geneva Declaration remained a continuing challenge with its simple statement: "The child that is physically or mentally handicapped must be helped."

World War II, despite its horrors and destruction, led to beneficial knowledge: In this context this relates particularly to a new understanding of the immense potential for rehabilitation of physically and mentally disabled human beings. Something else beneficial emerged from the holocaust of World War II: a new concept of the dignity of every man, woman, and child. And so, on December 10, 1948, the General Assembly of the United Nations adopted and proclaimed the Universal Declaration of Human Rights. It sets forth that no one shall be subjected to inhuman or degrading treatment, a provision which takes on special meaning for those who know the evils perpetrated at some residential institutions for the mentally retarded. It sets forth the right to education, to equal access to public service, to the right to work.

Notwithstanding the strong impetus generated by the Universal Declaration of Human Rights, there was considerable sentiment to come back and reformulate in more contemporary terms the Geneva Declaration. However, it was not until 1959 that the United Nations General Assembly did so by adopting a revised and expanded version and proclaiming it the Declaration of the Rights of the Child. Of the 10 principles of this Declaration, one, Principle 5, states: "The child who is physically, mentally or socially handicapped shall be

---

[1] Adopted by the United Nations General Assembly on December 20, 1971.

[2] The International Union for Child Welfare was created in 1946 by the merger of the Save the Children Federation and the International Association for Child Welfare.

given the special treatment, education and care required by his particular condition." Seen in this context, the International Leagues adoption in 1968 of the Declaration of General and Special Rights of the Mentally Retarded can be linked to, and undoubtedly is a product of, preceding international efforts. This, in turn, explains why it has met with such favorable response at the United Nations.

But no matter how forceful this international Declaration is, its provisions must be implemented on a national basis. The distinguished secretary general of the International Society for Rehabilitation of the Disabled, Norman Acton, wrote the following in an editorial:

> The world is gradually, too gradually, coming to understand that the challenges of disability are not reserved to a special few, but confront a growing proportion of its people. No family is without need of some of the services provided to supplement physical or mental limitations. The effective delivery of those services is a major economic and social responsibility of each government, far beyond the resources of the individual family. Proper legislation, effectively administered and supported by adequate budgetary provision, is the only rational basis for the fulfillment of this responsibility.
>
> In the ideal future, the human rights of every individual will be protected by a society of people whose education and maturity of attitude have eliminated all forms of prejudice and discrimination, and assured equal opportunity for all. Evolution towards that ideal cannot, however, be left to chance—we must depend on law to protect human rights, and on administrative mechanisms to insure that the values set forth in the laws are promoted and, if necessary, enforced. (Acton, 1971, p. 1)

This paper outlines the practical problems which must be faced by the associations for the mentally retarded in promoting the implementation of the rights of mentally retarded children and adults.

The Right to Education

The problem which, in country after country, caused parents of mentally retarded children to band together in the 1940s and 1950s, was the refusal of school authorities to educate their children. Of all the deprivation and suffering to which these families were subjected, this refusal was the most difficult to accept. The prejudice that these parents sensed in their communities was so strong that in most instances they did not insist on public education for their children. Instead they began to organize classes under their own auspices or turned to private schools. Later, when the financial burdens of these programs became unbearable, the parent groups began to ask for public subsidies. Since, "beggars cannot be choosers," they gratefully received financial and other assistance from whatever ministry or department offered them. This partially explains the varied administrative arrangements under which special education, particularly for mentally retarded children, has been conducted in various countries. Another reason is that the more severely retarded children were thought to be "sick" and therefore were considered to be properly the responsibility of the departments of health for all their needs.

Eventually, as it became obvious that mentally retarded children were by no means "ineducable" as educators claimed for so long, parents and professionals in the field began to question whether these children had not the same right to public schooling as other children. However, the picture became further clouded when, in various countries, at the request of parents and friends of the mentally retarded, legislation was introduced authorizing special education for one or another specifically designated group of retarded children. While this helped some of the children, it tended to reinforce in legislators and public officials the belief that *the others* indeed were ineducable and therefore not of concern to the educational authorities.

A confusing and contradictory worldwide picture with regard to education of mentally handicapped children resulted from these developments.[1] From country to country, and indeed within a country from city to city or province to province, there were striking and often incomprehensible differences in the way retarded children were either admitted to or excluded from the educational system. Slowly, all too slowly, it began to be recognized that these administrative school practices often resulted in serious damage—physical, mental, and material—to the family as well as to the child, and constituted a gross infringement of their legal and constitutional rights. Furthermore, closer scrutiny revealed that decisions of far-reaching consequence for child and family were made on the basis of questionable information by individuals ill-prepared for this purpose, and that adequate recourse and even adequate information was not available to parents regarding the basis for the negative decisions.

Today a proper reading of the Declaration on the Rights of Mentally Retarded Persons and of the preceding Universal Declaration of Human Rights leads us to one clear conclusion: *Every* child, without exception, has a right to education, regardless of the degree of his mental or physical disability.

Interestingly, as we approach the problem from this point of view we find that in many cases the basic national constitutions already spell out such a universal right to education. In Latin America, for instance, Argentina, Chile, and Mexico were among those countries where a broad constitutional provision regarding the rights to education certainly should have assured schooling for the mentally retarded child. However, in this context, Rafale Sajón (1965) correctly pointed out that "while some Latin American countries have constitutionalized the rights of children and the protection of the family and of helpless persons, very few of these countries have created adequate tools to safeguard (implement) these rights."

Obviously, Dr. Sajón's statement implies a challenge to develop the missing tools, and the associations for the mentally retarded must meet this challenge. With regard to the denial of proper education, the associations should pursue a two-fold strategy: (a) They must make known as widely as possible that with regard to meeting the educational needs of the mentally retarded children, we have now arrived at a new and radically different knowledge base. (b) They must learn to utilize the administrative, legal, and constitutional instrumentalities (actions) in their countries which permit a citizen to press his claims against local and national government.…

Much of this new knowledge is, of course, known to progressive educators. The strategy problem is to make it widely known to the educational profession in general, as well as to administrators and to the public at large. Individual countries need to be reminded that UNESCO instituted in 1968 a special education program. Governmental requests to UNESCO for aid, consultation, and training concerning schooling for mentally retarded children are now possible.

---

[1] For excellent documentation see (a) *A study of the legislation concerning the special education of handicapped children and young people* (UNESCO Document ED/MD/8, November 17, 1969); (b) *A study of the present situation in special education* (UNESCO Document ED/ME/16, March 15, 1971); Dybwad, R. F. (Ed.). (1978). *International directory of mental retardation resources* (Rev. ed.). Washington, DC: Department of Health, Education, and Welfare, President's Committee on Mental Retardation.

The second strategy—invoking administrative, legal, and constitutional remedies to protect the mentally retarded child's rights to education—is more difficult. In this regard, differences between countries are wide and generalizations difficult. Nevertheless, it is essential to try in various ways to inject the issue of the *rights* of the mentally retarded child when dealing with the authorities. The history of jurisprudence is replete with examples showing that in such matters the initial defeat carries within it the seeds of eventual victory. In other words, only by continuously and energetically asserting the rights of *all* retarded children to education can one expect to win eventual assent by the authorities....

The Right to Work

The right to education is interrelated with the right to work. Education is considered a way to help a person towards self-fulfillment, to utilize his capacity. For most people, this means being usefully engaged in a work activity. This is a problematic and largely unexplored area in the field of mental retardation. There are those, for instance, who feel that the mentally retarded person should be protected from having to work. It is argued that he may become exploited and that since he is already disadvantaged by being handicapped, we should not also expect him to work. However, the proponents of this view have never made clear what activities they propose for retarded persons in lieu of work.

Others maintain that the more severely handicapped should not be expected to work because of their feeble condition. Yet accumulating evidence points the other way—a regular, appropriate work activity enhances rather than endangers the retarded person's physical well-being.

In some countries another consideration comes to the fore: Parents feel that if their mentally retarded adolescent child receives vocational training leading to employment (even under sheltered conditions), this may endanger his eventual qualifications for invalidity benefits. A peculiar stratagem has resulted in several countries: In order to protect the mentally retarded person's right to invalidity benefits, those who have assumed responsibility for his care are unwilling to grant him the right to work.

It appears safe to predict that there will be a change in attitude among those working in the field of mental retardation or human welfare in general as well as among the families, since there will be continued comparisons between the physical, social, and emotional well-being of the working mentally retarded with that of the unoccupied mentally retarded. We can expect an increased understanding of the provision of the Declaration on the Rights of Mentally Retarded Persons, which states: "He has a right to productive work or other meaningful occupation."

Yet understanding is not enough. Society must make it possible for the retarded person to exercise this right. Sheltered workshops, for instance, must have some support from the state to secure work. Unfortunately, in many countries there are sheltered workshops which have everything but a sufficient amount of work opportunities. Without governmental action leading to legal or administrative provisions to safeguard work procedures for severely handicapped persons in sheltered workshops or in other sheltered employment, the right to work will remain an empty phrase for many retarded individuals. But government should do more than develop measures to increase employment opportunities. Associations for the mentally retarded must insist that government itself hire mentally retarded persons, just as it should hire individuals with other handicaps. Retarded adults who are working should have earnings commensurate with their productivity; this means, of course, that for the more severely disabled, the earned wage will be insufficient to pay for their maintenance. Therefore, Article 3 of the Declaration states: "The mentally retarded person has a right to economic security and to a decent standard of living."

This looks like a distant goal in countries where tens of thousands are starving and have no roofs over their heads. But there is no reason not to begin with countries which *do* have a high national income and yet do exclude the mentally retarded from many benefits, such as financial assistance commensurate with commonly accepted standards in the community.

The Right to an Appropriate Place to Live

The mentally retarded adult should have the right to leave the parental home for an appropriate residence home or an appropriate residence in the community—appropriate, of course, for his level of functioning. Obviously, this kind of arrangement is tied closely to an advanced state of industrialization. But even in industrialized countries, denial of suitable housing for mentally retarded persons is a new concept of prejudice. Prejudice is almost always related to ignorance; as in the case of education of the retarded, a priority task is to make widely known that in various countries even severely retarded individuals have demonstrated their capacity to live in small group homes and apartments in the community. Only thus is it possible to counteract effectively the widespread belief that (for their own good) mentally retarded adults are best cared for away from the community in overprotected institutional surroundings.

The Mentally Retarded Person as a Citizen

Those who work in the field of mental retardation should make an effort to speak as much as possible of the mentally retarded *citizen*. This will reemphasize the basic concept emanating from the Stockholm Symposium that the mentally retarded person is entitled to all the rights of citizenship unless, through appropriate legal procedures, it has been determined that there is a sound basis for specific abridgement of certain rights. Jose Eguia (International League, 1969) pointed out that this new concept implies also a revision of guardianship practices. Both in terms of graduation of the degree of tutelage and in terms of the guardian's role in protecting the personal interests of the mentally retarded individual against undue intervention by those responsible for his care....

The Mentally Retarded Child's Right to Live With His Family

In most countries, there is little doubt that a young child's most basic right is to live and grow up in his family home. For a small but nonetheless significant number of mentally retarded children this right is denied when they are confined in an institution. Often institutionalization is either initiated or supported by physicians under circumstances which are open to serious question. In many cases, a physician may recommend institutionalization "for the good of the family": Frequently, this means saving the parents from social embarrassment, but what about the right of the child? He is not a thing that can be disposed of like property (as used to be done with slaves). In other instances it is the lack of community facilities and services or the attitude of the public or certain professions—rather than the need of the child—which causes his confinement. Frequently a decision is made to send a child to an institution or hospital (which easily may become a lifetime banishment) without due consideration by the physician and the participating authorities of other solutions which would interfere far less with the child's basic rights. We are dealing here with a phenomenon that is highly unusual, if not unique, in the practice of medicine. For example, there are many medical administrators of mental retardation institutions who are convinced, who indeed "know," that they are receiving in their institutions children with mongolism who are actually harmed by being in the institution. Yet, year in, year out, these administrators continue to keep these children with mongolism confined (and I am using this term advisedly) in these institutions without so much as an official protest. Where in the field of medical practice would one find a parallel to this situation? (Dybwad, 1964).

The Right to Medical Care

In many countries, the severely and profoundly retarded child is being excluded from service in health centers and clinics for no reason other than that he is retarded, even though their medical services would be appropriate for him. One of the hardest and most heartbreaking problems encountered by parents is the lack of interest in, if not outright rejection of, their mentally retarded child by the pediatrician or general practitioner, even though the medical services he is requested to render are well within the province of his practice (Dybwad, 1968). There is also no justification for general hospitals to refuse admission to mentally retarded children merely because of their mental handicap.

On the other hand, the distinguished president of the International League of Societies for the Mentally Handicapped, Mme. Yvonne Posternak, a microbiologist at the University of Geneva, has called attention to questionable practices in the use of mentally retarded children and adults for medical experimentation—a clear case of the violation of basic rights. In this context, the International League's Stockholm Symposium referred specifically to the mentally retarded person's right to preservation of his physical and psychological integrity.

Involuntary sterilization would be a case in point, but fortunately reports over the past 10 years have indicated a sharp reduction in this procedure in both Europe and North America.

The practice of euthanasia must also be mentioned here as an attack on a retarded child's right to live. While there has been relatively little discussion of it, the topic continues to appear sporadically. It is noteworthy, for example, that the 1971 International Symposium of the Kennedy Foundation (Choices on Our Conscience) was introduced by a film showing how a newborn infant with mongolism (Down syndrome) was allowed to die over a 15-day period. In this case, the parents refused to give permission for simple surgery to correct an abdominal obstruction. In their opinion, any child with mongolism was better off dead than alive, and no one defended this child's right to live. At the Symposium many participants, including physicians, strongly condemned the hospital's failure to afford this infant life-saving medical treatment. It should also be mentioned that in one of the South American countries the impetus for the movement on behalf of retarded children came from an indignant father whose physician had suggested withholding life-saving antibiotic treatment to a little boy with mongolism with pneumonia. The father insisted on his son's right to treatment and from this clear confrontation gained an understanding of the broader issues.

The Rights in Balance

This paper has highlighted selected issues in the implementation of some of the rights of the mentally retarded. I must reemphasize for those not acquainted with the two documents that both the Conclusions of the Stockholm Symposium (International League, 1967) and the Declaration of Rights deal specifically with ways to ensure the rights of mentally retarded persons through proper legal authority.

It is undeniable that in the field of mental retardation the cruelties and superstitions of medieval thinking are still reflected not only in popular beliefs but also in public life and legal provisions and processes. There are, of course, striking differences from country to country as advances in knowledge promote a better understanding. Yet, all too frequently, one encounters remnants of the old views which essentially denied the mentally retarded person basic attributes as a human being, and, in many ways, treated him as a nonperson and social menace....

We are still in the early stages of recognition and implementation of the rights of the mentally retarded. Considerable work remains to be done over a substantial period of time before we can expect a general acceptance in society of these new concepts. Certainly, the associations for the mentally retarded have a significant role to play.

However, safeguarding the rights of mentally retarded children and adults can only be done by an association which is effectively related to the public life in the area in which it wishes to function—be it the local community, the state or the nation.... In the long view the role of the associations must be that of the spokesman, ombudsman, the advocate, for the mentally retarded child or adult—clarifying his rights and insisting they become a reality.

PART 3

EARLY INTERVENTION

Editors' Introduction to Part 3

It is very important to recognize that parents inspired basic changes in the field of mental retardation, now recognized by all. Most of the parents who led the rebellion were parents of school-age children; while other children went off to school, their children with mental retardation stayed home. These parents were being denied a basic right of most parents, to be relieved of the care of their children for certain hours during the day. Many of their children ended up in institutions because their parents could get no support for keeping them as members of the family.

During the middle part of this century, parents were not supported by pediatricians—the health care professionals they were most likely to visit during their child's early years. Pediatricians were not active with children with retardation; psychiatrists oversaw those services that were available. Even though people with retardation were seen as eternal children, psychiatrists were not in the business of children. Adult psychiatrists had no particular interest in the population and no training or insight into services.

In these speeches Dr. Dybwad makes his case for providing services for people with retardation while they are children, giving them opportunities to grow and develop in ways that other children grow. He encourages the service system to recognize that opportunities exist to support families as whole units. Families that are supported can provide training and stimulation to encourage and facilitate the child with retardation to be all that he or she can be.

Chapter 9
Why Does Early Intervention Come So Late?

Excerpts from a presentation at a seminar, The Young Child With Down Syndrome: Principles of Comprehensive Care and Stimulation, at the Children's Hospital Medical Center, Boston, June 1972

The question…is "Why does early intervention come so late in our efforts to develop services to the field of mental retardation?"

I would submit to you the following list of suggested reasons, not necessarily in order of their importance.

1. Paul Pearson, then the first chief of the mental retardation branch in the U.S. Public Health Service and now director of the Children's Rehabilitation Institute, University of Nebraska, wrote of "The Forgotten Patient" (1965). Having surveyed the literature on physician's role in mental retardation, he stated:

> The doctor's traditional concern for his patient seems to have been displaced by his concern for the parents, the patient's family or even the community. In other words, once the initial diagnosis is made and the retardate is neatly classified, the role of the physician as it pertains to treatment becomes focused on the parents. If one believes what is being written it would almost seem it is the parent rather than the retardate who is deemed to be in greatest need of treatment.
>
> This is not to question the need or importance of counseling for the family but rather to point out what I believe to be an important area of neglect. That is the need for the physician's interest beyond the initial diagnosis and classification and parent counseling. First, in the prevention and correction or at least amelioration of physical handicaps so as to permit the full achievement of whatever functional potential may exist. Secondly, even where no improvement in function can be foreseen, increased personal comfort of the patient and increased ease of attendant care must be considered as sufficient indication for medical and surgical intervention. (p. 917)

2. Certainly as far as Down syndrome is concerned, the physicians who are acknowledged leaders in the field all but ignore early intervention even in a narrow medical sense. Thus, reading the leading general treatise on Down syndrome by Penrose and Smith (1966) or the proceedings of the 1969 International Symposium on Down syndrome under the auspices of the National Foundation of Infantile Paralysis, a physician would get no inkling of these children's urgent need for vigorous and comprehensive early intervention. Nor does the American Medical Association (1965) handbook on mental retardation for the primary physician furnish him with any better orientation.

While the recently published and widely acclaimed volume by Koch and Dobson, *The Mentally Retarded Child and His Family* (1971), has a very useful section on the nurse's role in early intervention, the book has no equivalent section for the physician's role. In other words, a general practitioner interested in responding to the quest for early intervention would find little guidance in this otherwise valuable book.

As a matter of fact, last year's publication of the American Academy of Pediatrics, *The Pediatrician and the Child With Mental Retardation* (1971), is the first to carry a brief but informative chapter on health services. Attention must also be called here to Paul Pearson's excellent article "The Physician's Role in Diagnosis and Management of the Mentally Retarded" in *Pediatric Clinics of North America* (1968) and to the most recent volume of this series where our hosts Drs. Crocker and Cushna have a most useful and great contribution entitled "Pediatric Decisions in Children With Serious Mental Retardation" (1972).

3. There is an amazing ignorance regarding the applicability to early intervention of knowledge in the area of child development such as pertains to sensory stimulation, speech development, socialization (transposing, for example, the research of René Spitz re infant isolation), the role of play and of toys, etc., etc.

4. One encounters frequently what I can only describe as a psychological block against acknowledging the *possibilities* of intervention techniques for fear of promising parents too much (and thereby withholding help from children). This is a rather puzzling matter and reminds me of the opposition some of our professional colleagues have had regarding certain preventive public health programs in mental retardation.

5. There is also frequently observable, a cultural block on the part of the parents against having "outsiders" like public health nurses or early childhood educators come to the home. The reasons here are not easily ascertained (it may be an anachronistic hold-over from "My home is my castle"; it may be the peculiarly American idea that while everyone else may freely lean on a multitude of public, semipublic, and voluntary services, the mother of young children has to show her mettle by managing without public aid) as witness the peculiar rationale of President Nixon's anti-day-care manifesto.

6. Obviously, many services of early intervention would have to be rendered to the home and there we face a double handicap. Bureaucracies prefer to have the service seeker come to them—"We don't make home deliveries" is a national pattern by now (and no obstetrical pun is intended!)—and the helping professions themselves, such as social work, medicine, education, and physical and other therapists, excepting, of course, the public health nurse, have for a variety of reasons adopted a "come to see us in the office" viewpoint.

7. Finally, there is that peculiar American and in particular Massachusetts phenomenon: the edifice principle. We are told time and again—it is a constant refrain with my colleagues at the Mental Health Department—that the only way the legislature will give you money for personal services is in connection with erection of a building wherein this personnel will work. Yet what we need for early intervention is primarily personnel and not new buildings….

I have tried to sketch out some reasons for the widespread failure to deliver services of early intervention to very young children and some measures that might be taken to counter this situation.…Are we really opposed to giving little children, particularly helpless handicapped children, all the help we could give? Is there not some misunderstanding somewhere? We all *do* love children, you know—

Some of you may have read some of the contributions to professional literature by Robert Perske, formerly supervising chaplain at the Kansas Neurological Institute and now executive director of the Greater Omaha Association for Retarded Children. He has written eloquently on the "dignity of risk" and other aspects of the normalization principle.

Bob Perske attended the Kennedy Foundation's symposium and awards ceremony in Washington last year when the film was shown which depicted the fate of an infant with Down syndrome who needed minor surgery to overcome an intestinal obstruction for which the parents refused to give permission, so the child was left to die over 15 days.

In some ways this puzzling event is related to the puzzling phenomena I have discussed here today and so I want to ask your indulgence for closing my remarks with a bit of verse Bob Perske wrote after viewing that Johns Hopkins film.

WORD FOR A DOWN SYNDROME CHILD

We didn't want you,
helpless child of fifteen days
you were in the way,
So we shoved you into a corner…
    and let you starve to death.

No one wanted you,
Helpless child of fifteen days
Not your parents,
    Nor the helping professionals,
        Nor those who speak for God,
            Nor men using their wits to uphold justice.

Why didn't we want you,
Helpless child of fifteen days?
    Would you have stood in the way of our mad chase
        after the ideal family?
            (Which none of us will ever achieve.)
    Would we trip over you as we raise higher
        the GNP as our Holy Grail?
            (We must be "Number One" you know.)
    Is it because we have never learned
        to live graciously with our failures?
            (Failure is such a hard thing to face.)
    Is it because your less-than-perfect presence
        reminds us that we all have drives to
        "be something"?
            (We never want to be "a nothing.")

You bothered us,
Helpless child of fifteen days
We had to reject you
Because you made too obvious something in ourselves
That we just didn't want to face.[1]

---

[1] This poem was written by Robert Perske in response to his first viewing of the film *Who Shall Survive?* shown at a Joseph P. Kennedy, Jr., Foundation symposium on October 16, 1971. The poem was published in a local ARC newsletter, March 1972.

CHAPTER 10
THE MENTALLY HANDICAPPED CHILD UNDER FIVE

A presentation to a group of parents—Oxford District of the National Society of Mentally Handicapped Children, Oxford, England, September 1966

During the past 15 years we have made tremendous strides throughout the world in the field of mental health, in regard both to mental illness and to mental retardation or mental handicap as you call it in this country. There has been more progress in the last 15 years than during the preceding 50 years….We have made great strides in providing for the older children, for the young people, and increasingly also for the other retarded, but throughout the world the group which has been most definitely neglected are the youngest children, not just the preschool children in the general sense of the word, that is, those of nursery school age, but right down to infancy. Therefore we shall discuss here the needs of these children and how to meet them.

Case Finding

One of the reasons why these services have not been provided rests with the problem of finding those who need them. The reason we are beginning, in most countries, to provide large-scale programs at school age is simply related to the fact that at school age, in all civilized countries, we come, for the first time, face to face with the total child population. In the younger age groups, we may have some voluntary services of nursery school and day care centers, but the further down we go the less efficient mechanisms we have for really dealing with these age groups in large numbers. Thus, our first problem is case finding. How do we get to know the families with very young retarded children? One of the fictions you can read in many of our professional books and articles is that we can only find as very young children the most severely retarded, while it is said of the group generally called mildly retarded (you refer to them as ESN), that we are not able to locate them until they come into school or have been in school for a year or two, then fail, and then we pick them up.

This may superficially appear to be a correct observation of how things are, but a quite incorrect and actually quite unwarranted statement as to how things could be. The more we provide the right kind of nursery school services and the more we provide, at an earlier age, services to young mothers and their infants, the earlier we will be able to identify these children—thanks to our increasing knowledge about human behavior and its deviations, and especially about the reactions of infants in their bodily development as much as in their emotional, social, and intellectual responses. I am not going to elaborate on this; I merely want to point out to you that in this area of case finding we already have many problems that need to be solved and to which we must direct the attention of our research workers. We definitely should be able to discover children who need our attention before we let them linger in an educational system in classes that are not prepared to serve them, resulting in a great deal of frustration for the child and as much for the family and the teacher.

Now, of course, in the case of the severely retarded child, the initial case finding is easier. The question is what happens after the case is found, and here, unfortunately, we have a problem of communication. How do we communicate what is happening nowadays to professional people who have long left the university or other places where they were trained? Because many of the people who see the young parent who has a severely retarded child—the obstetrician, the pediatrician, the nursing personnel, the almoner or social worker, and so on—unfortunately are usually most inadequately informed of what can be done today for these children, their initial reaction to the parent is to say nothing. That is number one, a negative case finding—a case has been found but nothing has been said or done about it. Or we have another type of case finding. Here a case is found, but the parent is told, "Just wait, this thing may grow itself out." In the third and very frequent type of case, the parents are met with a great deal of sympathy and offered every possible consolation and moral encouragement, but nothing is conveyed to them as to what can be *done* for the child, and so, although the case is found, nothing really happens because nothing really has been set in motion. This case finding continues to be a serious problem, not only with the mildly retarded where we have not yet developed the proper mechanisms to identify them, but also with the more severely retarded where there is identification but nothing sufficiently useful is taking place.

After case finding comes diagnosis, which cannot possibly be discussed here in detail; it would carry us into theoretical considerations that would not be of great interest to you. Let me emphasize one point: It is not at all always necessary to provide the parent with a detailed diagnostic statement. Indeed with our present state of knowledge very often even the best of clinics cannot give one. What needs to be given to the parent is some practical information, such as, "Here is a child with special needs, and you can do thus and so about these needs." This is far more important for the parent to know than just the fact that the child is bestowed with a condition that has a strange-sounding Latin or Greek name.

Services

Now, what kind of services should be provided for the children under 5 years, through proper communication with the various professions dealing with this problem of early identification and diagnosis? First of all, parents need to know something about the problem they are facing. A lot has been talked and written about the emotional disturbances one finds in parents of mentally handicapped children. This is often the kind of emotional disturbance that would hit anybody, because it is an emotional disturbance as a result of uncertainty. If any one of us here in this room has to meet any kind of life situation with a sufficient degree of uncertainty, we become uneasy; if this uncertainty lasts long enough, we become increasingly uneasy, until our own breaking point is reached. *I want to underline that the greatest source of emotional disturbance of parents is this uncertainty—just not knowing what has happened—just not knowing what can be done.*

Parent Education

Therefore, I am putting at the very beginning of my list of needed services *parent education,* not parent counseling and certainly not therapy. First comes parent education, because parents have got to know: What is mental handicap and what is mental retardation; what is the difference? Why do we say one day mental subnormality and another day mental deficiency? What does it mean to my child? Is this curable, incurable? What can these children learn? What do experts from the various professions know today that would entitle them to make predictions for me? What are some of the needs of these children, and above all, in what ways are they like other children (rather than *un*like other children)? Thus, parent education is the first step—straightforward, good, sound education on the new principles we have developed about learning, exactly the kind of methods we are using now in business and the professions to convey new information to people. This can be provided quite easily, and it should be one of the main responsibilities of the public departments working in this area.

Counseling
Of course parents face problems of management, and those will differ very distinctly from family to family. It makes a lot of difference whether you live in a city or in a village; whether you have many other children or whether this is an only child; whether you are an older couple having had a lot of experience in raising children but not knowing what to do with this one, or whether this is a first child. There are many problems: It may be a situation of resentment by the brothers and sisters or interference from other relatives or neighbors, and so on. These kinds of questions still do not call for therapy; they are in the area of counseling, either individually or through group counseling, where parents can get together and discuss with skilled persons some of these problems which are general enough to be discussed in a group and yet specific enough to provide needed assistance to the parent.

Psychotherapy
Naturally parents of mentally handicapped children are as much subject to emotional stress and strain as any other group, and so among them too there are those who indeed need psychotherapy, possibly because long-standing friction between husband and wife comes to a head under the impact of the birth of a retarded child. In this type of case, of course, we may need to call on psychiatric assistance.

The important point I am making is that these are three completely separate processes: parent education, in which we provide information; parent counseling, in which we deal with some generalized problems; and finally psychotherapy when psychiatric intervention is needed.

Practical Help
Particularly for the young parent of the severely and profoundly handicapped child, information and counseling is not enough; what is needed is also practical help with specific problems of management. This is, of course, especially the case with children who have a combination of physical and intellectual handicaps and with whom it is often not easy to determine how serious the intellectual disability is until the physical infirmities have been dealt with. This home management help can be offered in many forms of service, by many types of personnel and under the auspices of different agencies, depending on the local situation, but this is undoubtedly a primary field for the profession you call health visitors (in other countries called public health nurses) who can concern themselves with aiding the mother with such important tasks as feeding the child, managing sleep problems, the handling of the child who is spastic or has other physical disabilities. The health visitor does function with a certain degree of independence in her

day-to-day work but never without the direction of a physician, and in this type of case, competent pediatric consultation is especially needed.

The health visitor will also need to consult a nutritionist, not merely for choice of diet but also for help with other feeding problems: children who do not swallow or children who have tremendous difficulty in moving on from a liquid to a semisolid and finally to a solid diet. This is a problem of such magnitude in families that it is really unbelievable that the health professions have, for such a long time, all but ignored it. In my travels I have encountered case history after case history where mothers have spent as much as 5 full hours a day trying to feed a severely handicapped child simply because nobody told them the "tricks of the trade." And if a mother who has other children spends 5 hours a day on feeding her severely retarded child, it is merely a matter of time before this family explodes. Unfortunately, our health visitors as yet have not been trained sufficiently in this area, but the knowledge is there to be taught. Books and slides are available with illustrations on procedures they could learn in five easy lessons, but because they have not yet been taught this, they are not helping the parents in this area.

Family Help
This is as good a place as any to mention something else and that is the strange notion, which even very intelligent people constantly reiterate, that we really cannot afford to do so much for retarded children because we have to worry first about normal children. Well, I do indeed worry about the normal children in a family where the mother spends 5 hours a day feeding the severely retarded child. In other words, retarded children do not live in isolation somewhere; they live in families, and to the extent that the parents have to spend an undue amount of time and money on the retarded child, the family unit gets interrupted and disrupted. In such situations it is obvious that the so-called normal children are damaged far more severely than the profoundly retarded child, whose sensitivity, unfortunately, is so encumbered that he is not so aware of what is happening. So please challenge anybody who puts forth the idea that we cannot afford to help families with severely handicapped children, because we first have to help the normal children. It is on account of the normal children in the family, born or as yet unborn, that we must be particularly worried about such things as feeding problems. By the way, a very excellent report was recently published in London on what happens to families with severely retarded children. It is entitled *Mental Subnormality in London—A Survey of Community Care,* and I strongly recommend it to you because it gives very excellent examples of the difficulties faced by such families.

These nutritionists are very important, and so are home economists, to give these parents some management help: how to organize a household with a severely handicapped child, how to work out schedules, where to purchase special clothing, and so on. Obviously we need the health visitor, and a physiotherapist should also be on the team at least for consultation. All this should proceed under the advice and guidance of the physician, but we cannot possibly expect busy physicians to concern themselves with these problems other than to give direction.

Guidance in Child Development
As essential as these professional workers who can aid with the child's physical problems are, we need still another type of person. Retarded children have a different and very often irregular pattern of growing up, so the

guidance they need from parents has to be of a special nature—a more intensive guidance, a more definite helping along. Most people in this room know how hard it is to guide children in general: They sort of run away from you; they walk before you have time to tell them how they ought to be doing it; they are off on their first motor-bike ride before you ever have a chance to warn them why not to do that. Children grow so much by themselves that, when faced with a severely retarded child, parents do need the help and the consultation and the comfort of talking with somebody who knows something about learning and growing, someone who can reassure them but also very definitely keep them from pushing too fast or, still more likely, not pushing enough. Thus we do need guidance in the home for the parent with a very young retarded child—also in terms of his development in acquiring the skills, abilities, and aptitudes that young infants develop through their stages of growth. You will recognize that this type of professional worker really hardly exists; what is needed here is a child development worker, a specialist in infancy and early childhood education—using the term education in its broadest sense, beginning with the earliest stimulation of cognitive responses of the child.

Home Help

There is something else parents need. You cannot expect a mother with a severely retarded child (and even a mildly retarded child if there are other children in the family) to be on deck all the while. Your country has pioneered for many decades the home help service, women who can come into the home to take over the household duties, be it once a week so that mother can at least go shopping in peace and quiet, or more frequently if there is a really severe problem. The home help or home maker service assists the family in managing this problem of having a severely retarded child by giving the mother just enough relief to enable her to carry her heavy burden and to keep the child in the home and in the family unit, at least during early childhood. Obviously both the form and substance of the service will differ substantially depending on whether we deal with a specific management problem or whether we are dealing with general deprivation in the social-economic problem area.

Short-Term Care

Let me go on to another type of relief for the families with children under the age of 5. Some of these services are already established and are projected to be increased in your community, but I want to spell them out for those in the audience who may not so much use them as help pay for them. We must provide relief to mothers by day care services, whether for a few hours or all day. In other cases night care may be needed, such as where a mother is able, willing, and eager to have the child during the day with her, but, particularly with an overactive child with sleep problems, at night there is just too much disruption in the family. Weekend and vacation care is needed at certain occasions or just plain emergency care, because the mother is sick. By offering these services, we will very often avoid the necessity for the vastly more expensive continuous care in an institution.

Now I realize that there are some people who always carry on some strange arithmetic with regard to their pants pockets. If the money comes out of one pants pocket, they think it is much less than if it comes out of the other pants pocket. But ultimately you all are the taxpayers, regardless of whether a service is under one jurisdiction or another. If you can avoid full 24-hour care over long periods at state expense and instead have a partial service on a local basis at a much lower cost, you all have gained very substantially. Therefore, you have to look at the total cost of this problem at a long range, and consider that these new programs of day care, night care, weekend care, emergency care can make the difference whether a family can themselves shoulder the responsibility or whether they are forced to ask the public to take over the care of the child. This is a very important point, a lesson in practical economics.

Baby-Sitting

Another service which many people do not take seriously enough as yet, but which is developing into a real community service, is baby-sitting. There are now communities which have trained baby-sitters—young girls and older women—for handicapped children. They have taken a course and have been given instruction as to what they may encounter with a severely handicapped child. They know how to deal with a spastic child or one with seizures; they have learned when one has to call a physician, and so on. Availability of this service is so necessary in this day and age of migration when we no longer have Grandma and Aunt Emily in the same town. Increasingly industrial firms shift their workers around on the map and more and more we find young families all alone in a community without the traditional family resources on which to call for aid in "minding a child." That is why the community must step in and provide this service.

Pediatric Care

Now I come to a more difficult problem, and that is the general unavailability of adequate pediatric care to parents of severely mentally handicapped children. This is an international problem. Somehow still today the majority of pediatricians and family physicians are not interested in taking care of these children on a day-to-day basis—though they may be interested on a theoretical basis, in reading articles and following research reports. But they do not seem to relate this to the actual health needs of these children.

Part of this puzzling state of affairs is explained by a long-standing medical superstition that mental retardation is primarily a psychiatric problem and, therefore, not the business of the pediatrician or family physician. I have just come from a consultation visit in a country where this is well exemplified. When a mother comes there to the mother-and-child health center with an infant afflicted with Down syndrome (mongolism), she is automatically told that she must seek help from the Mental Health Service of the state. But when she goes there, she finds no help because her child does not need a psychiatrist but good child health care, and specific guidance from the pediatrician or general practitioner. We encountered exactly the same situation in another country. If you wonder to what extent this is a problem in England just take a look in what neglected health condition children of 5, 6, 7, and 8 years are admitted to services offered by the local health authority or the regional hospital board.

What we need for the very young severely retarded child is good health supervision, more intensive supervision naturally than for the child without such problems, but health supervision that is very much along the procedures of ordinary maternal and child health centers. We are dealing with feeding difficulties and other problems of the child's growth and development which should be the daily bread-and-butter activity of the physicians there. Many of these children have disorders in their sensory apparatus with vision, hearing, and so on that should be attended to already in infancy. There may be a problem of cardiac involvement, a disturbance in the digestive system, spasticity, and any number of infirmities that could be remedied or ameliorated but all too often are not being attended, and as a result children frequently are quite unnecessarily further handicapped beyond the unfortunate disability with which they were born. I know this is not a medical audience, but here is a problem which concerns all of us. How you can press for its solution is something you have to consider from your knowledge of your own community and of your own country, but action is needed.

Down Syndrome

Let me come back as an example to the child with Down syndrome. It is most distressing to see how many of them are inadequately nourished by being kept on a soft (baby food) diet and, therefore, are not exercising their jaw and mouth muscles which are crucial to the development of language. Thus the basic language deficiency which all these children show is further complicated by this faulty dietary management, simply because the mother does not have the benefit of continual adequate health supervision for the child. A similar problem for children with Down syndrome is the need for weight control, a typical child health supervision procedure. Why should we allow these children to develop an obesity which particularly in later life will prove to be a major obstacle to their social adjustment, but which already during their early childhood unnecessarily interferes with active play and, that means, needed social contacts with other children? Children with Down syndrome have serious dental problems (again aggravated by inadequate diet), yet they typically receive less dental supervision and care than normal children. Poor motor coordination, poor muscle tone, deficiencies of vision and hearing, and of the upper respiratory tract are other typical health problems of the child with Down syndrome. All have long been proven to be open at least to substantial amelioration if proper medical attention is provided, resulting in a considerable improvement in the child's response to education and rehabilitation.

Speech Problems

Speech problems are, of course, not just typical of the child with Down syndrome; they constitute perhaps the outstanding deficiency common to most retarded children. Unfortunately parents all too often neglect to encourage speech development; with more severely retarded children, they become so discouraged with the child's lack of response that they assume he will never learn to speak, and as a result they talk less and less with him. They need therefore the guidance and encouragement of someone who knows about speech development and can demonstrate to them appropriate ways of speech stimulation, seeing to it that the child hears a lot of speech, that speech is directed at him. At a later stage an expert may decide that there is also need for specific speech therapy, but that is another matter. Certainly in the area of speech development we face a tremendous challenge with the mentally retarded under the age of 5.

Lessening Dependence

All the supporting services I have discussed, beginning with parent education, will bring to parents assistance in the management of the mentally handicapped child, such as in toilet training, sleep habits, eating habits, choice of food, adequate physical exercise involving both small and large muscles, appropriate play activities, toys, and speech development. Very important also is training toward lessened dependence—in particular accustoming the child to be away from home. It is amazing how many retarded children have never slept away from home and how many have never been away from mother for more than 5 minutes. Therefore, I do want to emphasize that with retarded children who are slow to progress and to get used to new situations, it is particularly important that parents are guided in preparing the child to be away from mother—to be away from home. Of course this needs to be done slowly, so they can get accustomed to this in small doses. Unless we enable the child to be prepared in this way for a separation, we quite unnecessarily provoke a crisis for him, which in turn provokes a crisis for the mother, when at a given age he has to be away from home and is not at all ready for this. So here is another very important consideration for children under 5. One mechanism for doing so, which does not cost the ratepayers any appreciable money at all and does not have to wait on the construction of buildings and hiring of staff, is guidance to parents of retarded children in organizing small informal play groups for three or four other children, which can meet in the families' homes or in some other suitable location. In the beginning they might meet only once or twice a week and for only short periods, but this will cut through the social isolation of these children which constitutes for so many of them an additional handicap. As the play group progresses, one or two mothers can take over, so that the other mothers can go shopping or have a peaceful cup of coffee while the children thus get used—in an environment to which they are getting accustomed—to have mother go away for an hour or two. At first the children may do no more than play by themselves, with the other children present in the same room, but slowly some limited group play and group interaction may evolve, resulting in a readiness for entrance into nursery school or kindergarten.

Nursery Schools
I do hope that in this city which has taken the leadership in developing nursery school services for the normal child, you will consider to what extent you can accept some handicapped children in these nurseries. This has been done very successfully and if it were not so late I could read to you some very interesting accounts from South Australia where on a statewide basis all nursery schools and kindergartens are cooperating in accepting handicapped children, so none has to accept more than it can easily absorb. Obviously it has only good effect if a few handicapped children, prepared for this experience, can be integrated in a normal nursery school or kindergarten.

Who Am I? The Self-Concept
I would now like to refer briefly to another need of children under 5. This is the development of a self-concept and a self-image. Normal children easily progress through a series of natural growth experiences which builds up in them a sense of self. Retarded children not only are slower to perceive, to learn, but their cycle of experiences is more limited. They need more learning opportunities and instead usually get less. Too often there is failure on the part of adults to accent the individuality of these children. The questions "Who am I?" and later "What can I do?" give a clue as to what we need to build up in them. Obviously a degree of realization of one's being handicapped will be crucial for the self-image of the older child and adolescent, but with the under 5 retarded, the accent must be more on "What can I do?" I have also been interested in seeing how some progressive mental retardation institutions have used individual and group photographs and slides to develop in the children a body image, which, of course, is an indispensable part of one's self-concept as a person.

Physical Fitness
As a final point, I would like to underline the need to be more concerned with fitness of all retarded children.

Here again the physicians should take the leadership and convey to parents the great importance of this. Of course we have had traditionally some very destructive attitudes. What did we used to do with TB people? We put them in a sanitarium and made them neurotic. What do we do with TB people today? We put them to work and keep them active. When a young child had a serious operation or illness, he used to be excused from physical exercise and gym, when just the opposite was needed. It is just the same with the retarded children; they need more rather than less physical exercise than the normal child. Now it is of course difficult to guide them in this, but this is why parents need professional assistance to know how much they can ask of their child.

This emphasis on physical fitness is not just for the purpose of improving the health, stimulating the appetite, and so on, but there is a very important other factor in this. So far nobody has given us the slightest hope that we can improve the brain substance once it is impaired. We only can give these children a greater capacity of using what brain substance they have. However, we can definitely help them to overcome their other physical disabilities in many ways through appropriate medical steps as well as through training. We can give them the best possible skill in throwing a ball, and what will happen when they know how to do this? They will be more acceptable to other children, and when they are more acceptable to other children, they will be in more social contact, and when they are in more social contact, they will in turn be stimulated socially by these other children to the extent that they are capable of absorbing more. So, therefore, physical exercise is not just a health measure as far as these children are concerned, but very specifically a step toward social acceptability.

Label the Services, Not the Child

I would now like to make one further comment, because when I read the annual report of your society I was made aware that you have become involved with the present controversy as to who should administer and supervise educational services for the severely retarded. I agree with your implied position—I think it was more than implied—that eventually we must come to the point where medical services are administered by competent medical authorities and educational services are administered by education authorities.

However, there is one sentence in your report to which I want to take strong exception, because it reflects the kind of thinking which has created a lot of confusion from the Ministry of Health up and down. Your committee has, of course, pondered long and earnestly the question of who should care for the severely mentally handicapped child. Here again it is not a matter of sharp division, but your committee is confident that it will be possible to distinguish between those children who can profit from education and those who are in constant need of nursing care. This is the sentence: "That the severely handicapped children must remain the responsibility of the Ministry of Health has never been disputed." This is what I want to dispute. What is wrong here is the thought that the Ministry is responsible for any child. No ministry should be responsible for children. Families are responsible for children, and when no family is available somebody else—a person—but for heaven's sake not some anonymous office in some ministry. This is a totally wrong concept. Ministries are responsible for services, and as soon as you recognize this, your whole problem is solved, because to the extent that a child needs health services, the Ministry of Health and the local health authorities will provide it; to the extent that a child needs education services, then proper education authorities will provide it; and to the extent that the child needs both, then both will have to be involved. This is the crux of the whole problem with which you have been struggling so long in your country. Similarly do not talk about ESN children, do not talk about SSN children—talk about children who need ESN services or SSN services. Children may need one type of service now, and yet after we have given them this service for some time, they may be able to profit from a higher level of service. Label the services and not the child and your problem will solve itself to the extent that it will enable you to make the proper administrative determination.

Chapter 11
What Went Wrong?

Excerpts from a presentation, "The Mentally Retarded in the Changing Society," at the Third Asian Conference on Mental Retardation, Bangalore, India, November 1977

As one who has been active in mental retardation in the United States for almost 40 years, I sympathized with President Kennedy's statement that when it came to mental retardation, the United States was still a developing country. At the time many of my colleagues disagreed with Mr. Kennedy, but subsequent events have shown quite clearly that much of what was then considered by my colleagues as solid knowledge substantiated by research has since been found faulty.

What went wrong with our research in the United States? I, for one, think that we were too impressed with the exactitude of our research techniques and not sufficiently aware of the *in*-exactitude of the data on which the research was based. And still today a great deal of the research that is now taking place deals with attempts to evaluate and often justify the deficient services and facilities of the past and is, thus, of little consequence to developing countries.

If there is one overall, broadly applicable factor that has emerged from the work during the past decade or two, it has been that universally the capacities of mentally retarded persons have been underestimated.

However, it is not my intention to put all the burden of our failures on our colleagues in the field of research. In many cases it has been the misapplication of research findings that was at fault. And this brings me to a point of caution I wish to emphasize very strongly. Not only do we face a changing society…but within the society the life situation and the status of the mentally retarded individual are undergoing a steady change.

Therefore, great care has to be taken in utilizing research findings and survey figures based on old data and observations. This is particularly important as we project future programs for mentally retarded adults. The considerable body of knowledge we have about their limited community adjustment, about their need for supervised living arrangements, their inability to sustain a satisfactory level of effort in a work situation, their difficulties in handling money, their problems in communicating with others—all is colored markedly by the fact that few, if any, of these adults had an adequate school program; few, if any, had stimulating environments; few, if any, had parents who received positive guidance about their retarded child's needs. Indeed, many of the parents of this older group had been advised that their son or daughter would not develop into adulthood and would remain "childlike." Consequently, the life experiences vital to the process of growing up were held to a minimum, and consequently this information tells us much about past practices but little about future potentials.

In contrast, we have now been able to observe how early training can help preschool children with substantial intellectual handicap to handle social relationships, to achieve communication skills, and to develop a capacity to function with less dependence on parental protection. We are now beginning to see young people whose stimulating time of growth in preschool was followed by experiences in school and home that systematically provided them with continued opportunity to develop life skills. While the ultimate outcome of such careers has yet to be demonstrated, the sheer extent of activities open to this coming generation of retarded adults makes it necessary for us to reassess our planning strategies all along the line.

The words *all along the line* bring us face to face with what I see as the most urgent challenge in this field: early intervention. A review of the literature, of government and agency reports, makes it very clear that even in countries with extensive networks of mental retardation services, relatively little programming exists to aid the very young retarded child and his parents. My wife and I verified this 2 years ago when we visited a number of European countries with generally advanced social programs just to find out to what extent such a policy had been translated into general practice. This is astonishing from two points of view. On the one hand, from many countries we have a mass documentation from parents describing the pain and suffering of the early years with their retarded child when they looked in vain for solid information, helpful guidance, and practical support in coping with their retarded child's problems. On the other hand, there has been widespread recognition of the significance of the early years in the development of the child. I am, therefore very pleased that a recent document from the World Health Organization (1977) and a report by the U.N. secretary-general made to the Commission for Social Development of the U.N. Economic and Social Council (1975) both emphasize the need for earliest intervention.

I am keenly aware that for some countries in Asia, in Africa, in Latin America, where even the most basic child health services are only spottily available as yet, a proposal for early intervention in mental retardation may sound like bitter irony. However, it is necessary to remember that the initiation of any governmental program is almost always preceded by a long-range planning effort, and a major step toward planning is the recognition of a need and of ways to respond to that need. In this regard, developing countries have the great advantage of being able to learn from the mistakes that have been made in the past by countries which by and large started their mental retardation programming with the school-age child. Even in countries with extremely limited resources, it is possible to initiate a modest program of early intervention which can be based on omission rather than commission (i.e., by *not* passing on to parents of newborn children with obvious defects the kind of unnecessarily negative, misleading, and discouraging information which in the past has so deeply disturbed countless parents and set off a chain reaction very damaging to the child).

A next step in early intervention (which again is quite feasible in countries with limited resources) is to prevent development of policies which would exclude the child with mental retardation from generally available services, for example, the basic child health station. In this connection an Eastern Mediterranean Region Conference held in Cairo in June 1976 recommended "early detection in infant welfare clinics together with straightforward advice and counselling" (World Health Organization, 1976b). The problem almost automatically mentioned when such proposals are discussed for adoption by developing countries is the unavailability of suitably trained professional workers to carry out the tasks. Therefore, your attention should be called here to an important World Health Organization (WHO) publication entitled *The Primary Health Worker* which includes a relatively brief section on mental retardation (World Health Organization, 1976a).

All the recent international reports that have come to my attention and many statements from professional agencies in the field have emphasized our need to recognize in more realistic fashion that in most cases of mental retardation, regardless of severity, the natural family represents the strongest force in the process of rehabilitation and training.... For most of the countries with long-standing mental retardation services this implies a distinct shift away from previous practices which tended to tell parents there was little they could do for their retarded child. This view led to the building of massive institutions so as to relieve parents of the care of their retarded child and to the present paradoxical situation, particularly obvious in the United States, Canada, and Great Britain, where the maintenance of these large mental retardation institutions, built under the old philosophy, has become so exorbitantly expensive that funds are hardly available to initiate the much more effective system of providing support to these families so that the child can remain in the community.

While there continues to be a vocal group which insists that there will always be a need for the large residential institution in the field of mental retardation and that parents want to rid themselves of the burden of caring for a retarded child, I have observed, having worked closely with parents of mentally retarded children in many lands throughout the world, an increasingly strong disagreement with that view. So it is of significance that the 30th World Health Assembly, in their plenary session of May 18, 1977, resolved to urge member states "to accord adequate priority in their health policies and development plans to actions that will prevent mental retardation and provide necessary care and support for mentally retarded individuals and their families, mainly through non-institutionalized community action" (World Health Assembly, 1977).

Significantly, this links up with the work of yet another WHO unit, the Expert Committee on Child Mental Health and Psychosocial Development, which, when meeting in Geneva in 1976, made one of its main recommendations to "involve families in treatment and seek to increase parental skills and competence." In other words, early intervention through collaboration with parents relates strongly to the growing emphasis on the role of the family and the home environment as the focal point of efforts to cope with mental retardation. Whether in the extended or in the nuclear family, it is the normally expected affection, family bond, and security of the home environment and the guiding hand of the parent which are increasingly, albeit belatedly, recognized as the keystones in individual programming, and as of such value that financial support to parents caring for a severely handicapped child is seen as a legitimate public expense.

Once we can establish effective aid to families with retarded children, we will have to depend less and less on the traditional mental retardation institutions or hospitals, as some countries have chosen to call them. I know that my views are very controversial. But I am a patient man and ready to wait until the results of early help to families will have established its effectiveness in preventing the need for institutionalization....

As a former administrator of a state child welfare program, I am, of course, aware that not all families can be expected to deal with their severely handicapped children in their home. However, when this occurs our effort must be to find another suitable family setting. I realize that this may not be within the reach of a developing country which has not yet established a child welfare program. But this point needs to be made strongly, lest a country, under the pretense that it cannot find substitute family care, undertake the building of large institutions with construction and maintenance costs per child by far exceeding what would be involved in a family care placement.

One final point about the significance of early intervention, and that pertains to the close link to efforts in prevention.… Let me just state here that aside from broad-scale socio-economic measures to improve the basic living conditions (food, shelter, employment, etc.), our best chances for primary, secondary, and tertiary prevention of mental retardation center on improved maternal and child health care, as does so much of early intervention.

An effective system of early intervention must have organic links to the system of primary education and is, of course, affected by the present trend to provide preschool education at an even earlier age. While there are striking differences from country to country even in Europe, the trend is unmistakable. As education recognizes increasingly its responsibility to deal with developmental problems of substantially handicapped children as early as possible, the educator, social pedagogue, nursery teacher, or child development specialist must be a member of the early intervention team.

…There is no longer basis for questioning that *all* retarded and otherwise handicapped children, regardless of the severity of their problem, can benefit from schooling. We must clearly recognize that the fallacious and prejudicial term *ineducable* referred to lacking skills in the teacher rather than to inability to respond on the part of profoundly handicapped children. The grotesque situation of looking to welfare or health authorities to provide learning opportunities for retarded children is fortunately not only put under question but actually being discontinued in country after country. It is one of the strongest demonstrations not only of the changing place of the retarded child in changing society, but also of the changing state of our knowledge about the processes of learning and teaching.…

CHAPTER 12
THE REDISCOVERY OF THE FAMILY

From "The Rediscovery of the Family," 1981,
Mental Retardation, 32 *(1), 18-36, reprinted with permission*

Much of the severe difficulty faced by families with handicapped—and, in particular, severely and profoundly handicapped—children is due to unnecessary deprivation, neglect, and rejection suffered by these families beginning practically at birth. Hence, a prime factor in the support that must be developed is early intervention. We must begin at the beginning. The beginning will bring us to the delivery room, or in some countries to the midwife, and to the moment when the mother is first made aware that she has given birth to a child with a severe handicap. Nor should we forget the way in which the father first learns what has happened and the suggestions made to him.

When things go well at birth, the shifting of responsibility and guidance to the parents from the obstetrician to the pediatrician and the supportive role of the nurse present no great problem. But the literature is full of countless testimonials that when a child is born with marked impairment, the situation is quite different, and the parents, still today, are all too often left in ignorance or, worse yet, with inappropriate information, injurious to them as much as to the child.

In my travels to many countries, I have learned to pinpoint this problem by posing a simple question which I can ask in Banares, India, just as fittingly as in Quito, Ecuador, or Miami, Florida: "In your community, when a child is born with a serious impairment, immediately recognizable, such as Down syndrome or spina bifida, what happens? Who tells what to whom, and how is this initial message translated into appropriate action in support of this particular family, without any damaging delay?"

Because of my frequent travels, I am, of course, aware of some of the bright spots, the islands of excellence. But what we should be looking for here for the future is a *system*, a system which will assure that the family is enabled, right from the start, to develop its own resources in meeting the needs of the new arrival.

The essence of early intervention, of course, lies in making available to parents not only advice and counsel but detailed technical instruction, or perhaps specific equipment that will help them in taking care of their child and furthering growth and development (Caldwell, Bradley, & Elardo, 1975; President's Committee on Mental Retardation, 1975). From our own experience with many parents, we know, for instance, that feeding such a child may pose great problems, taking hours of the mother's time and causing her great anxiety. Yet there are simple ways of helping the mother to teach her child to suck, to swallow, to chew. Specially constructed spoons or cups will greatly aid the mother, and I am forever amazed at how little known are the excellent publications, slides, and film strips which demonstrate how parents can teach their children these most essential life skills (Massachusetts Department of Mental Health, 1973)—essential not only for the physical growth of the child, but also to reduce the time the mother is occupied with feeding the child, so often to the detriment of other children. But from the point of view of the family as a mutually supporting entity, I have come to believe that one of the most crucial elements in the acceptance of the severely mentally handicapped child into the family unit rests in his having acquired eating skills and eating behaviors, so he can share in meals at the family table. From this one shared experience, from the child's sense of accomplishment and from the satisfaction of the other family members, brothers and sisters as much as parents, will grow his participation in an increasing number of family activities.

Too often, we are overprotective in dealing with young handicapped children, and overly concerned that we make too many demands. The concept of "the dignity of risk" as developed by Robert Perske (1972) may appear to be too sophisticated in terms of the infant and very young child; however, the pattern of activities which allow the young child to experience a certain amount of risk and failure needs to be set very early.

The services that the family can most effectively provide to meet the developmental needs of their child must be supplemented by relief that is brought to the family, which in the most severe cases, even during the child's infancy, should not be expected to carry the entire burden, 24 hours a day, 7 days a week. The kind of relief will depend on the cultural and societal situation and can be more easily arranged where the large, extended family still can be found.

However, are there not families that simply cannot cope with a handicapped child, even if they are offered and have tried all essential helping services? True enough, but true also that there are families which for other reasons find they cannot cope with a nonhandicapped child. In any case, when this occurs, we must recognize that this is a problem for the family and children's agency, public or private, because our priority now must be to find for this child a different family setting, whether by foster care or adoption. Such action would not be taken rashly, but we cannot grant to any family the right to exclude their child from the development and emotional benefit of growing up in a family home.

Obviously, the extent to which this can be accomplished depends on the level of functioning of the handicapped person, but as I have pointed out before, that, in general, has been greatly underestimated.

Of significance in all of this is the sense of identity we all have as members of families. Here again, we need to pay particular attention to persons with more severe handicaps who, as many of you must have observed, have hardly ever heard their family name spoken; yet a name is a priceless belonging, as are family pictures, and as are brothers and sisters, even though they may live in distant places. Indeed, the International League has a task force, consisting of brothers and sisters of handicapped persons in many lands, which is exploring just these issues I have mentioned.

Any discussion on future developments in mental retardation needs to proceed from a recognition of the inherent strength of the family to deal effectively with the needs and problems in the development of a child with mental retardation, provided the community is ready and willing to lend its support.

It is necessary to acknowledge that this deviates distinctly from assumptions and beliefs commonly held until recently. They were thought to be based firmly on scientific evidence and professional experience which now have been proven erroneous and must be discarded.

Parents have a natural tendency to look after their children, handicapped or not. The gross exceptions that do occur merely underline the general rule. There is ample uncontradicted evidence in the literature of many countries that it was as a consequence of inappropriate counseling from professional sources and the community's unwillingness to render assistance that parents concluded they were unable to cope with their severely handicapped child. And, as a consequence, there has been built up a massive apparatus of services (not limited to institutions) to substitute for family care. It is only natural if from within this massive service system based, in general, on public appropriations, we encounter resistance to change.

When a severely handicapped child's condition requires intensive medical or very specialized therapeutic approaches, they can best be carried out in appropriate community facilities (hospitals, pediatric nurseries, rehabilitation centers, etc.). As has been amply demonstrated in England, Canada, and the United States, institutionalization of handicapped children in the traditional large state and provincial multipurpose institutions can and must be avoided. There are no services available in the mental retardation institution which cannot be performed with equal or better adequacy and economy in the community.

Emphasis on the family and on the roles and rights of parents does not exclude an equal emphasis on the rights of the child with mental retardation. The parents' basic rights are inherent not in parenthood, but in personhood and individual citizenship, similar to those of the child. In case of conflict, these rights need to be put into balance.

Just as professional workers have underestimated parents' capacity to deal effectively with the rearing of severely disabled children and built this assumption into the existing service system, so they have underestimated the inherent capacity of the child, adolescent, and adult with severe disability for growth, for a meaningful place in their family built on maturity, for a steady lessening of their dependency, for participation in society, for self-expression and self-determination....

Part 4

The Role of Professionals

Editors' Introduction to Part 4

Initial efforts to provide training to people with disabilities, as exemplified by Samuel Gridley Howe and Dorothea Dix, were limited. While society was willing to look favorably on such small-scale "experimental" training efforts, it was not at all prepared to generalize this perspective and view all people with disabilities as having the potential to be productive members of the community. The only profession interested in dealing with people with retardation was psychiatry, and early psychiatric efforts focused on pathology, not learning; on diagnosis, not appropriate treatment or services.

In the early days, parents of children with mental retardation were considered a problem by the psychiatric profession and by society in general. It was assumed that they somehow contributed to their child's retardation, and it was further assumed that they lacked the capacity and the neutrality or balance to help their children effectively. For people with retardation in the early decades of this century, there is ample documentation that at best they were considered a nuisance and at worst, a menace to the well-being of the family and the community at large.

Psychiatrists knew best, and their advice and experience influenced the developing system of services. The evolution of the institutional model is a direct response to the "problems" posed to society by people with mental retardation. As new professions developed to respond to the needs of people with retardation, they were guided by the philosophy of the time: that professionals, particularly doctors, knew best about working with people with retardation, that parents had no particular wisdom to offer, and that people with retardation were passive recipients of services designed and provided by others. To view parents of children with retardation as people with rights was foreign; to consider that people with retardation had rights was unthinkable.

In Dr. Dybwad's view, rights of individuals with mental retardation continue to be denied. Rather than as leaders, professionals must come to see themselves as partners, with parents and with people with retardation. For professionals to play a vital role in the future, they must first give up their own prejudices: They must see people with retardation not as an alien subgroup of society but as a valuable and important thread in the social fabric. Dr. Dybwad was among the first in the field to demand that the rights of people with mental retardation and their families *must* be the foundation upon which services are built.

CHAPTER 13
TOWARD HUMAN RIGHTS FOR THE MENTALLY RETARDED: A CHALLENGE TO SOCIAL ACTION

Excerpts from a presentation to the Social Work Division of the American Association on Mental Deficiency, San Francisco, May 1969

With your permission, I would like to…try to discuss with you some of the action implications which present themselves today to social workers in the field of mental retardation in general and specifically to those working in residential facilities, in the light of the recent draft statement of the revised Standards for Social Services Departments in Institutions for the Retarded, just presented to our [American Association on Mental Deficiency (AAMD) Social Work] Division for consideration.

The theme of the AAMD conference this year is Social Issues and Social Action. It is a challenging topic and one to which all of us are ready to respond, and the draft document appears to fall well in line. In its first section, entitled "Philosophy," is set forth that:

> The social worker will decide in each problem situation whether his attention needs to be directed toward internal difficulties experienced by the individual, toward the process of social interaction, toward the relevant environment, or some combination of all three. Intervention in order to be effective needs to go beyond the maintenance of the status quo. Changes may be desirable in social organizations and institutions as well as in individual and family functioning.

In Section IV, entitled "Indirect Services," the second paragraph reads as follows:

> Social service engages in appropriate activities to see to it that its policies, plans and administration lead to the realization of its goals in the most effective and efficient manner possible. It contributes its particular expertise to the making of policy, the planning and the administration of the residential facility as a whole. It engages in evaluation of its own programs and those of the residential facility and fosters timely program innovations and development.

Let me say here in all sincerity that last spring I most likely would have been quite content with these formulations. Here were certainly all the words I had come to accept as beacons toward a more adequate recognition of broad social issues and the action pattern required to meet them. But then something happened to me last fall. I encountered for the first time as university teacher a group of the young social work students. Those of you who heard Vice-Chancellor Billingsley yesterday will remember his reference to the new dynamism young people have brought to our universities. Perhaps I can best compare their first impact with a sudden breeze coming through an open window and blowing one's paper about, annoyingly disturbing the orderly process of one's accustomed daily work. One hears from those young students slogans such as "lack of relevance," "advocacy," "establishment," "rights," "protest action," which sound quite familiar. One wonders at first what all the noise is really about. But then, lo and behold, one discovers that far from "sloganeering," these young people are trying to communicate to us not just their concern, their growing discontent with what they see on the social scene, but also their grim determination to veer away from our traditional ways of doing things which they consider ineffectual, toward some new action patterns which to them have promise of coming at least closer to the mark. They are not so much seeking to create conflict as they are seeking to confront effectively the existing conflict situations which we have tended to avoid. Their allegiance does not lie with the profession. They want to relate directly to the people in need and feel they have common cause with them against an establishment which they think is as eager to suppress their motivation as it is to keep the client in a state of dependency.

This is not the time and place to dwell at length on the phenomenon of the student protest; let me just say that I, for one, have been deeply impressed by our young students' sincerity of purpose, their commitment to action, and their skill in ferreting out the inefficiency of present methods, and in developing not only new strategies but also new and vital allegiances with groups which until then had merely been *objects* of concern.

Let me remind you that a year ago, at AAMD's annual conference in Boston, Whitney Young admonished us that too long had we been interested in methodology and techniques rather than in social impact. He emphasized that the leaders in the movement to eradicate chronic injustice and poverty in this country should be those people who have benefited most from the American system, and he ended by quoting the Greek philosopher who said, "We shall achieve justice in Athens when those who are *not* wronged are more indignant than those who are" (Young, 1969)....

Our young students have shown considerable acumen in identifying these organizational and bureaucratic roadblocks which interfere with appropriate and effective action response to stressful situations.

Our young social work students are not content with merely stating that the new orientation in social work must stress clients' rights as much as clients' needs, they feel the obligation to give active support to, and work hand in hand with, Mothers on Welfare and the Welfare Rights Movement, organizations which have caused much stress, puzzlement, and fear in older workers and administrators.

And thus I return to the draft statement of the revised Standards for Social Services Departments in Institutions for the Retarded. Again stressing that I previously would doubtlessly have been willing to endorse this draft, with the insights I have gained from our young students I find this document wanting, because it obviously is more oriented to the maintenance of our establishments than to protection of the rights of individuals, and because it suggests that the retarded person be helped to learn the roles that will enable him to relate constructively to the formal and informal system within the residential facility, even though Robert Edgarton's study, *The Cloak of Competence: Stigma in the Lives of the Mentally Retarded* (1967) proves so compellingly how destructive this compliant role playing is to the individual.

I find the document wanting because it suggests that the social service department helps the family to develop trust in the residential facility and helps the family to engage in a *counseling* relationship in which they can explore and communicate troubled feelings and actions in relationship to the retardate and the residential facility, but it fails to recognize that there may be no sound basis for developing trust in an institution and that parents may rightfully resent being pushed into a casework-counseling relationship when they try to air grievances and concern about their child's treatment (or lack of it).

I find the document wanting because it speaks only of needs, not of rights, and because of its lack of recognition of the advocacy role social service must assume on behalf of the retarded person and his family rather than a mere "liaison" role as is suggested. I find the document wanting because it not only fails to recognize the advocacy role of the social worker but fails to take any cognizance of the existence of associations for the mentally retarded which on their part have played a far-reaching advocacy role, granted that this has been done in some localities with less effectiveness than in others.

The strange lack of responsiveness of the social work field in general to the problem of mental retardation, even in the face of extraordinary manifestations of public interest, has been documented elsewhere (Dybwad, 1969b). Let me merely add here that the lack of reference to the associations for the retarded in this draft document reflects a widespread tendency on the part of administrators and professional workers, particularly those in institutions, to look upon these associations as little more than donators of birthday parties and needed equipment the state fails to provide....

We face a strange phenomenon in this country. On the one hand, a presidential committee for 2 years in succession has criticized in strongest terms the inhuman treatment to which individuals in many of our state institutions are exposed (President's Committee on Mental Retardation, 1967, 1968). To the contrary, we are over and over assured that once we get more money to hire more staff and repair some buildings there is not much to worry about. Those of you who know the conditions in some of the California institutions must, indeed, have marveled at the nonchalant attitude with which the director of the California Human Relations Agency, Mr. Spencer Williams, glossed over the very conditions which are a matter of such deep concern to the President's Committee and, of course, to countless parents and informed citizens who know so well what Mr. Williams professes not to know. We must recognize, of course, that Mr. Williams's task is in the political area. But what about the [local] social service departments and their professional responsibility?

What is their responsibility in the face of flagrant violations of a resident child's or adult's human rights that come to their attention? What about willful concealment of the true nature of a child's death or serious injury, caused by gross negligence of the institutional staff? What about continuing exposure of young children to vicious sexual assaults because of the administration's refusal to take appropriate action?

What about the gross abuse of medication or other medical treatment which when used as a disciplinary measure without doubt constitutes cruel and unusual punishment, outlawed under the Constitution of the United States?[1]

Or the use of residents for peonage, involuntary servitude at long hours, again outlawed by the Constitution?[2]

---

[1] Bill of Rights Article VIII: Excessive bail shall not be required, nor excessive fines imposed, nor cruel and unusual punishment inflicted.
[2] Bill of Rights Article XII-1: Neither slavery nor involuntary servitude, except as a punishment for crime whereof the party shall have been duly convicted, shall exist within the United States, or any place subject to their jurisdiction.

What about denial or undue restrictions of visitation rights to parents, particularly parents from disadvantaged backgrounds who cannot effectively protest? What about measures deliberately designed to humiliate children, such as keeping them naked for punishment or placing a child or adult in a group functioning at a much lower level, again solely for disciplinary reasons?

What about the withholding of a child from schooling—an act which if committed by the parents would result in court action?

Who will be the child's advocate if not the social worker?

Who will convey to parents the true information, or see to it that it is conveyed to them, if not the social worker?

These are not hypothetical questions; I am referring to actual happenings in the recent past—not in one state but in several.

And thus it has come to pass last week that the Pennsylvania Association for Retarded Children (1969) having in vain communicated by letter, visits, and telegrams with the governor, the secretary of welfare, the director of mental retardation, and others to bring to their attention clear evidence of gross irregularities, including cases of negligence resulting in death of residents, decided in their annual convention by unanimous vote to authorize its board of directors to engage counsel to determine what kind of legal action may be taken to compel the state to remedial action.

Once again, the parent association and only the parent association came forth as advocates and defenders. Where was the Social Service Department? Safely barricaded behind the aforementioned roadblock that protects the bureaucracy in what is known to sociologists as system maintenance.

Who is being attacked? Who is the guilty party?

My friend and colleague Dr. Roland Warren reminded me just the other day that when an effort was made after Hitler-Germany's collapse to take to account the German industrialists who had made great profits from collaboration with Hitler's extermination policies, the point was made from our side that after all, these industrial leaders were all honorable men.

It is always so—"all honorable men." But the question still remains: What about those whose fate is entrusted to the honorable men—who will speak for them?

Chapter 14
The "Medical Model"

Excerpt from a presentation, "The Mentally Retarded in the Changing Society," at the Third Asian Conference on Mental Retardation, Bangalore, India, November 1977

As important as allocation of financial resources is the way in which we use and develop our manpower resources, and here, too, some definite changes have occurred. As long as mental retardation was seen as a kind of mental illness or as a problem subsidiary to the field of mental health, facilities and services were developed in the image of the "medical model." Institutions servicing retarded people were called hospitals, although most of the residents were not ill, and the persons who looked after them were called nurses. A colleague of mine, a physician in the Austral-Asia region, with many years of experience in the field of mental retardation, wrote me only recently about his concern that so much emphasis is placed in this part of the world on medical and particularly psychiatric services in the care of mentally retarded, on beds, clinics, and institutions, and especially on university training schemes for high-powered "experts." My friend's concern relates to the fact that while at least some of the parents of retarded children may have the privilege of a consultation with the expert, they have great difficulty finding a physician who will look after the basic health needs of their child on a continuing basis. Unfortunately, as World Health Organization (WHO) pointed out again last year, many medical schools provide no training at all in dealing with children or adults with mental retardation, and the few that do, concentrate on gross clinical abnormalities found in institutions. Even in countries with fairly well developed services, one still encounters parents who cannot secure for their retarded child eyeglasses, hearing aids, and even needed surgery because the physicians do not think one should "bother" with a retarded child.

What is needed, on the one hand, is to make basic health care and good child health services available to all retarded children, and, on the other hand, to inject into medical training current information adequately reflecting the potential of persons with mental retardation.

Jakob Oster, a Danish pediatrician, has some significant recommendations in this regard on the basis of a study he undertook a few years ago on medical training in mental retardation, in which he demonstrated that in many instances the kind of information the physician receives in medical school actually impedes the development of a positive attitude toward retarded persons.

Nor is this a problem just with the medical profession. Psychologists, social workers, and educators similarly display frequently a rather negative view toward the person with mental retardation, which clearly goes back to long-outdated, prejudicial information, unfortunately still taught in the universities and printed in the textbooks. While I am always ready to support and participate in efforts to tell the general public about new developments in mental retardation, I see a far greater need to bring about a better understanding of mental retardation on the part of the profession just mentioned, because it is they who not only influence public opinion but often make decisions which exclude mentally retarded people from services. To understand the seriousness of this information gap, one has to have a grasp of the tremendous progress that has been made during the past two decades. And, of course, I need to underline here that the progress has been made possible by individual members of these disciplines and professions who often had to work in isolation, and some of these thinkers, innovators, writers, and teachers are sitting among you in this room.

I am aware that plans are under discussion for regional professional training institutes in Asia, bringing in experts from other regions; having observed the workings of international scholarships for many years, my wife and I strongly favor a regional center as a way of reaching large numbers of persons and assuring that the learning which takes place will be appropriate in the country of the participant. However, regional training sessions do not negate the need for adjustments in the basic professional university training.

There is another area of concern in the training of professionals working in the field of mental retardation and similar handicaps. As I pointed out earlier in my presentation, the parents of handicapped children are playing an increasingly more active and significant role, not just in organizing societies to press for broader and better services, but also as individual participants in the planning and implementation of the developmental program for their own child. Many helpful books have been written and courses organized to give parents the information they need to assume these tasks. What is also needed is a *changed orientation* on the part of the professional worker to help him accept the parent as a member of the team, a full participant in the deliberations and privileged to receive information that once was considered the professional's prerogative....

Chapter 15
Parents and Professionals

From "The Rediscovery of the Family," 1981,
Mental Retardation, 32 *(1), 18-30, reprinted with permission*

More than three decades have passed since parents of children with mental retardation spontaneously banded together in many countries to demand justice for their children and an end to discriminatory practices denying them and their children access to services available to others in the community. As one who has worked in the field of mental retardation for 42 years, I can, from my own observations, testify to the truly revolutionary impact of this parent rebellion.

I need not review in detail the practical beginnings of the parents' campaign. Suffice it to say, it originated with rather small self-help projects undertaken by individual parents reaching out to others. It is interesting to note that this was not just the pattern in the industrialized countries of the West, but also occurred in strikingly similar fashion more recently in South Korea, for example (R. F. Dybwad, 1971).

Although the beginning usually originated with unilateral action by parents, once programs were under way, in most instances there was an outreach to professional persons, and conversely professional workers sought to approach the newly formed parent action groups so they could assist in the programs and provide professional guidance. I do not mean to imply that there developed a sinister plot on the part of professional workers to take over the programs the parents had initiated, but in the normal course of events, programs grew rapidly to fill the long-existing void, and that meant more and more professional workers became involved, and steadily things moved in the direction of traditional patterns of agency operations.

Some of this was related to the fact that parents were motivated to get for their children what other children were receiving and that was, of course, in the first line, schooling. Quite naturally, there was an early recognition that programs were needed after the school years, and so the occupation center and sheltered workshop program began to unfold. There developed, also, a large variety of subsidiary programs, play groups, recreation programs, but, in terms of overall effort and investment, they were quite secondary.

What needs to be stressed here is that the overwhelming numbers of programs were organized for children of school age and beyond; very few programs served the infant and very young child. As always, there were exceptions to this generalization. For example, in the late 1950s, a parent association service in Massachusetts made themselves available to other parents of newly diagnosed handicapped children to answer questions and provide counsel and support.

In the mid-1970s my wife and I visited a number of European countries with the specific purpose of finding out to what extent there were programs serving the handicapped infant and very young child. We found to our great surprise a dearth of effective early intervention, as these programs have come to be called, even in countries which in general were recognized as leaders in the mental retardation field (Dybwad, 1976).

My reference to the "Rediscovery of the Family" implies that the family somewhere got lost. How did this happen? Part of the answer lies in a peculiar phenomenon related to the strong existing prejudice toward the problem of mental retardation, particularly on the part of professional persons. In 1964 Dr. Paul Pearson, an American pediatrician, wrote a very significant article entitled "The Forgotten Patient" (1965) after having reviewed both medical practice and medical literature. He pointed out that physicians were primarily concerned with helping parents cope with the problem of having produced a child with mental retardation, but that little was done to help parents with the actual management of the child, to reassure parents regarding the potential of the child as a *developing* human being. In those days the general view of mental retardation was that it was a static, unchangeable condition, not just "once retarded, always retarded," but "once severely retarded, always severely retarded"—with a fixed IQ.

Social workers were primarily concerned with parental attitudes, and the literature abounds with articles ascribing to parents of handicapped children strong feelings of guilt and consequent psychological problems. Thus the social workers also felt they had to help the parents with these psychological problems. They failed to recognize that what was most upsetting to parents was that nobody was there to help them help their children; they failed to recognize the inherent strength of the family.

For the parents of a handicapped infant or a very young child, the much-publicized slogan "Retarded children can be helped" was but an empty promise until their child was getting ready for school, at which time service might be available, outside the child's home.

Edward Skarnulis, in trying to shed light on this situation, has referred to "the residential assumption" (1976). He points out that although the vast majority of persons with mental retardation do live in the community, and certainly spend their childhood years in the family home, there remains a pervasive assumption in the industrialized countries that persons with mental retardation do need (special) residential facilities just because they are handicapped. And this assumption persisted even though in these same industrialized countries the use of congregate residential institutions had long been discontinued for nonhandicapped children whose parents were unable to care for them.

Physicians, social workers, and psychologists were convinced that the mere presence of a mentally handicapped child in a family would prove detrimental to other siblings and constitute an unbearable burden to the parents. True, the situation was often tense, but primarily because parents were left without services, without guidance, without emotional support of any kind.

In most so-called Western societies, there has developed over time, in varying degrees, a value system which puts the person who has mental retardation at the very bottom of humanity, whereas a high intellectual functioning is considered at the opposite end of the scale, a greatly prized attribute. The extent to which the intelligence quotient has been used as a broad measurement of human value is very revealing in this regard. At first blush, this may seem a rather reasonable arrangement, but is not health a human condition of equal importance? Just consider what strange and paradoxical situations we would face in our societies if we would replace the IQ, the intelligence quotient, with an HQ, a health quotient, as an indication of human capacity and of potential contribution to society.

Underlying the residential assumption as highlighted

by Mr. Skarnulis is this perverted value system in which a person with mental retardation becomes grossly devalued. Indeed it has been proposed that the individual with profound retardation altogether lacks the quality of being "a person" (Dybwad, 1981).

Just as professional workers have made prejudgments about the family's expected attitude toward a handicapped child, so have they put before us time and again judgments as to the public's unwillingness to allow persons with mental retardation to live in the community. Yet as someone who has worked in this field for four decades, what has, in recent years, consistently surprised and delighted me has been the readiness of the general population, the neighbors down the street, plain folks, first to tolerate and gradually to accept persons with disabilities. To be sure, we have occasional troubles, but so do we have troubles in every phase of life, from the home to the church, to the market place and to our place of employment.

Today, not 1,000, not 10,000, but hundreds of thousands of substantially handicapped individuals walk on the streets or get about in wheelchairs, shop at the supermarkets, go to the movies, use buses and street cars, and go to ball games and playgrounds. They go to places where they never used to be seen, and yet the number of untoward incidents is minimal. We have here a clear example of how a new perception, observing one's handicapped neighbors, leads to acceptance. To use an old adage: Seeing is believing.

Let us not continue to project onto the families or onto the man in the street an unwillingness to cope with handicapped children and adults. To the contrary, I contend that these prejudices originate with my professional colleagues in psychology, social work, medicine, and the other so-called helping professions; and I would add the somewhat risky generalization that the higher the academic training my colleagues may have enjoyed, the more they are apt to impede persons with severe handicaps, individually and collectively, by restrictive views, by a low level of expectation, by a refusal to accept their educational or rehabilitation potential. I am well aware that these are grim words, but I think, with noble exceptions which always exist, by and large this has been the picture.

Let me be more specific: Over and over I have observed professional persons with advanced academic training who become not just uncomfortable, but actively angry and even hostile when they are confronted with substantial achievements of persons whom they consider as incapable of making progress....

I have dwelt at such length on this rather unhappy look into the past, because in bringing you a very optimistic view of the rediscovery of the family in the field of mental retardation, I also felt I had to be specific about obstacles we are facing in such a reorientation of our programming.

The key to this new programming was most succinctly expressed by Ed Skarnulis (1979). His challenge is simple and direct:

Support, not supplant, the natural home.

Part 5

Deinstitution-alization

Editors' Introduction to Part 5

Dr. Dybwad came from an institutional background through his work in the prison system, in juvenile corrections, and in mental retardation. His perspective began to change as he became active in the National Association for Retarded Children (NARC). In his first speech to this body in 1953, Dr. Dybwad urged the NARC to support the evolution of smaller facilities as a step toward community settings. He argued for training across the disability spectrum. And he provided the vision for NARC to move toward a "society without institutions."

Over the years from the early 1950s, Dr. Dybwad was part of a sea change that saw parents visiting their children in the parts of the institutions where the child lived, rather than in special visitors' rooms. He saw classes develop in which children learned functional skills and where play was an important part of the day. In the late 1970s, Dr. Dybwad was invited to visit an institution where he sat in on a case conference. To his delight, he saw the child's parents seated at the head of the table, contributing as equals with the professionals in the room as they worked together to plan for their child. This shift of power was of tremendous importance: For the young child, goals were being set that expressed the parents' interests in family unity and strength, that promised involvement in regular community activities, and that reflected the evolution of the parent from "cause of the problem" to "implementer of the solution." Quality of life assumed importance, and the recognition that quality was possible outside the institutional setting was a revelation. That true quality of life could be achieved only outside of institutional walls, and within the mainstream of community life was the next step in the developing model of services called community membership. Although these represented positive changes, Dr. Dybwad continued to assert the need for community based services as the only way that people with mental retardation could truly become members of society.

Chapter 16
Beginnings and Endings: The Quality of Life for Young and Old

Abbreviated version of presentation at the 10th Anniversary Conference of the New York State Commission on Quality of Life, Albany, May 1988

It was in 1938, exactly 50 years ago, when I began working at Letchworth Village, one of the older New York State mental retardation institutions, on a study of young residents who had been involved in delinquency in the community. I still remember my amazement to discover a procedure which gave me my first clue that those confined in that institution were treated in ways which at first seemed grotesque until it began to dawn on me that these people were not considered to be quite human beings like the rest of us. What I observed was simply this: Letchworth Village had one of the first EEG laboratories, and the entire population was being screened. Because some of the residents were restless, the laboratory technician positioned each on a table, and, to distract their attention, a Mickey Mouse film was shown on a small screen within view of the resident. The machine was shut off as soon as the examination was finished, maybe in the middle of the film, then turned on for the next resident. Once the film was finished it simply was played backward for the next person instead of being rewound. The technician, a kindly older man, said to me, "They wouldn't know the difference anyhow." And so Letchworth Village in those days had for the "people who wouldn't know the difference anyhow" dormitories overcrowded with 100 beds and 125 children sleeping in those 100 beds. I also actually saw in those early days an incontinent man in a small room lying in a box of sawdust. There was no bed. Still, Letchworth Village had a large medical staff, a well-staffed social service department, and was famous for its psychological research laboratory....

At the close of the 1950s Governor Clement of Tennessee came to the end of his tenure and one day told his staff that he would like to have a nice state building named after him. Somebody suggested that Cloverbottom, the state institution near Nashville, needed a new building for severely, multiply handicapped patients. The idea appealed to the governor, and he instructed the staff to spare no money. Shortly after the building was completed, I visited there and the superintendent, a well-known psychiatrist with experience in other mental retardation institutions, proudly took me to the new building. It was filled with cribs made on three sides of the best Tennessee marble, with an aluminum wire mesh front that opened. The crib stood high on four steel legs so the staff did not have to bend over. (And all that was needed was another marble slab on top to change the crib into a tomb.) But then the psychiatrist showed me the main feature: He called an attendant who came with a hydraulic jack on wheels, quickly lifted the rubber mattress with the patient on it, and rolled the jack to the middle of the large dormitory. There was a gangway there with low walls from which streams of water could be turned on so that as the jack rolled through, the patient was bathed, untouched by human hands.... The psychiatrist smiled with satisfaction, turned to me, and said, "This is our 3-minute car wash!"

Why have I told you these appalling vignettes of past institutional life? Because the system that created these dehumanizing arrangements is still with us today. To be sure, very considerable changes have been made, but some of the senior staff who worked under those conditions are still on the job, and we need to be mindful that by and large it was only as a consequence of outside pressure, especially from the courts, that the system finally and reluctantly discontinued some of these practices....

Chapter 17
The Undeveloped Resource at the Edge of Change

Excerpted from a presentation at the Fall Conference on Mental Retardation, cosponsored by the California Council for Retarded Children and the American Association on Mental Deficiency, San Francisco, November 1968

Your theme for today is "The Undeveloped Resource at the Edge of Change." If you listened with care this morning, you found that, undeveloped or not, this resource has an edge that is quite sharp and may cause some pain and, indeed, there may even be a little bit of blood.

Essentially we are here to talk about change and how much of it came and why more did not come. Throughout the United States one can observe isolated examples of very excellent specialized programs for the mentally retarded that have been in existence for many years, and yet, not only in the neighboring states but very often in the very same state, they have not been adopted or adapted by others.

A large number of professional workers representing many disciplines have written reports on outstanding services for the mentally retarded in other countries and have furnished elaborate documentation through the printed word, through photographs and slides. Numerous committees and commissions—and certainly you had no dearth of them in California—have reported on needs. As a matter of fact, I still refer back to some of the earlier reports from the California legislative committees which were far advanced, with sweeping recommendations for improvements. President Kennedy's campaign to combat mental retardation was, of course, of particular significance. President Johnson's Committee on Mental Retardation, in its report in 1967 and again in 1968, was no less critical than had been President Kennedy's original panel in 1962. Yet with all of this, progress has been amazingly slow.

Now I think it might be good if we stopped talking for a little while this noon as to *what* you *ought* to have, and try to find out *why* it is that you are not getting it. What are the obstacles to change? An overall national problem, brought out this morning, is the way in which society at large, communities, and also certain societal institutions still perceive the retarded as a deviant person. I think we have a long way to go before we can effectively change these attitudes. Every once in awhile, we get some very grim reminders such as the *Atlantic Monthly* article, you will recall from earlier this year, which advocated euthanasia for all children born with mongolism. Every once in a while, you get a glimpse at the depth of such feelings that still exist and which we conveniently try to overlook because we have a tendency to overlook the unpleasantness. Certainly this kind of role perception, as the sociologist would say, of the mentally retarded as a deviant person or, as that article suggested, a nonperson, is change inhibiting.

Another inhibiting factor is the sheer extent and size and monetary value and, last but not least, the economic utility for certain communities of the current physical plants, facilities, and services of the large institutions for the mentally retarded. They tend to block, or at least effectively delay, action toward change. This is again an unpleasant topic. We do not like to suggest that *people make money by building institutions*, all sorts of people, all sorts of money, money which is not made when funds are used to hire needed staff. Thus, certainly the momentum of the current service pattern centering on large institutions is another effective inhibiting force.

Looking at this problem from a broad or nationwide perspective, one can characterize the present development of mental retardation services in the United States somewhat as follows: Although there has been widespread advocacy for increased emphasis on nonresidential services, the need for residential services is perpetuated and reinforced by the placing of a low fiscal priority on nonresidential services and of a high fiscal priority on maintenance and, in many states, still on construction of residential facilities. The result is a shortage of nonresidential services, which of course, in turn, leads to an accentuation of the urgency for the creation of additional residential services, which are storing up an ever larger number of individuals since those ready to return to the community cannot be released, cannot return because of the inadequacy of funds for nonresidential services. Here is a real vicious circle all through the country, representing, I repeat, the momentum of the current service pattern. System maintenance is what this is called by the sociologists, who have become more and more fascinated with this phenomenon.

But then, of course, we have some other inhibiting factors toward change. Different groups have investments in different services, and certainly there are several professional groups that have a very substantial investment in the present institutional system. They are concerned with their job status, job security, job opportunities, and this is a definite inhibiting factor. About that there can be no doubt, because enough public documents have been released by the particular professional organizations to make quite sure they will lose neither their jobs nor their influence.

Yet another strong inhibiting factor is a very human failing: denial of reality. The need for change can be effectively repressed by denying unpleasant realities which would underline the urgency for change. When Burton Blatt, the head of the Department of Special Education of Boston University, undertook with a photographer friend to expose the shocking conditions in American institutions for the mentally retarded, and produced the book *Christmas in Purgatory* (Blatt & Kaplan, 1966), he was attacked. And this is not at all a rare occasion. Those who point at institutional atrocities will find themselves much more sharply attacked than those who commit them.

Even Sen. Robert Kennedy had the experience that the people of the state of New York had very little interest in listening to an account of the truly horrible conditions existing in a large state institution for retarded children located within the boundaries of New York City and serving some 5,000 people. And they were even less inclined to do something about it. Professor Sarason of Yale, in that respect, recently quoted, "eyes that see not, ears that hear not, minds that deny the evidence before them" (1969, p. 45).

There is another very interesting and paradoxical maneuver. We had a clear example of it in Massachusetts when the movie *Titicut Follies* was produced, depicting conditions in the Bridgewater institution. Let me assure you, this was a very fine, sensitive film which really was done with a very sympathetic eye and in no way exploited the situation in terms of showing individuals.

But in a paradoxical yet sanctimonious successful maneuver, the state administration protested against this invasion of the privacy of institution residents, thereby blocking effective exposure of institutional practices which result day by day in routine denial of elementary privacy and rights to dignity for the residents!

And then we have something else, a flower that grows particularly well in California soil, a kind of patriotism, state chauvinism, or even parochialism. The great state of so-and-so proudly proclaiming its preeminence in industry and finance, in culture and education, cannot afford to let it be known that with all its riches, its glittering state office buildings, its highways and freeways, it treats in its institutions human beings, as you well know, in ways a dairy farmer would treat his cattle.

When President Kennedy met for the first time with his Panel on Mental Retardation, he turned to the chairman, Mr. Mayo, and said "Mr. Mayo, what do we have to learn from foreign countries?" Mr. Mayo assured him quickly that the panel would send abroad some task forces. And in typical Kennedy fashion, this was the first question Jack Kennedy raised a year later when the panel submitted its report. With his phenomenal memory, he turned to the chairman and said, "Mr. Mayo, what *did* we learn from foreign countries?" Well, as you know, we learned a good bit, but strangely our administrators seem resentful about it and hesitate to apply it.

To say that California is remarkably advanced in the care of the retarded may be a nice attempt to please the governor, but it just is not helpful at all. And to be very frank with you, I thought in this morning's session we had some very bad instances of this. You were assured again and again that you are really quite good. Let me tell you, you are not! Let me tell you that there are smaller states that will show up much more favorably. One part of your problem—and 15 months ago I tried to convey this to you at the annual convention of the California Council a little bit less vociferously—is that you have and always have had a need to point out that really you are better than the others. It reminds me of the story of a woman who met the new Episcopal rector in town. She said, "Reverend, how are you?" And he said, "Well, I tell you, Mrs. Frank, I do not like things at all. Sunday the church is half full and at the Wednesday evening vesper service barely a handful of people." And she said, "You are so right, Reverend. You are so right. But the lord be praised, the Methodists are not doing any better."

Why do you have this hesitancy to admit that something is grossly wrong—a hesitancy, by the way, President Kennedy did not have? He very forcefully said, "Here is one field in which we are behind, and badly behind." I wish—and I am addressing myself to the California Council very specifically, as an organization—I wish you would have the courage of your conviction and not always have this bland and meaningless politeness, this reluctance to speak out.

Why do you not turn to the task at hand? We all love California. Yours is one of the most important states. Yours is one of the richest states. Yours is a state that has greater resources than most others, because everybody wants to come to you. So why should you, first of all, be content to compare yourself with others? But, secondly, why do you not take a closer look and really see what others are doing?

Fifteen months ago, when I met with you for the annual meeting of the California Council, I made a very few comments about certain unfortunate things at Sonoma State Hospital. The speech is taped. You can listen to it. I made no gross accusations or judgments. Yet the reaction I got was "That is no way to talk about our institution and the Nelson Building. Why did you have to do so at our dinner?" Well, Tom Nelson is a good friend of mine, but I cannot help that he allowed his name to go on a building which represents not only an outdated program idea, but, in addition, is a prime example of wasteful and damaging design, an architectural atrocity that has made you "famous" the country over.

Why is it that you cannot face up to these things? Why is it that you always have to cover up things with qualifying statements? I made one point 15 months ago: "Do not just blame the present administration for the predicament in which you find yourself. Because it goes back—far back." You know it. But you never admitted it in the past. And now when things really get rough, you are making some statements which I do not think are quite correct.

Yet things are, maybe, changing, I hope. I agree with Leo Cain that there *is* a difference between 1964 and 1968. The increasing confrontation we have in this country in many fields, the sharpening of issues, may perhaps help you to have the courage to come to similar confrontations in this area. Healthy controversy is of greatest help toward producing change. Vigorous exchange of viewpoints should never be impeded. And if you have the opportunity to discuss things in meetings like this and debate issues straightforwardly, you certainly should try and do so and not equivocate just to be polite.

After all, President Kennedy's panel spoke out very forthrightly that throughout the country the quality of care in our institutions was low, was highly objectionable. *MR 67*, the first report of the President's Committee on Mental Retardation, used much harsher words, saying, "Many of these institutions are plainly a disgrace to the nation and to the state that operates them" (p. 29). This year's report, *MR 68: The Edge of Change*, signed—may I say—by two eminent Californians, one of them sitting here and the other sitting in Los Angeles, said, "Many of the nearly 200,000 residents in state institutions for mentally retarded live in disgraceful conditions which the state's own regulatory agencies would not tolerate in private facilities"(p. 11). And, of course, I am mindful that one of the speakers today pointed this out and appealed to you to try and translate this into action.

If official government reports can use this kind of language, why should you have this terrible need always to be so desperately polite? You see, we are not attacking individual human beings. What we are talking about is a system, a system which, I repeat, has been in existence for a long time. You deal with an establishment, a bureaucracy, a professional power structure with various other power structures attached to it, and this cannot be blamed, when it manifests itself in any one location, on individual persons.

Dr. Vail, the head of the institutions in Minnesota for mental illness and mental retardation, had the courage to write a book entitled *Dehumanization and the Institutional Career* (1966), in which he mercilessly presents a detailed documentation of the many ways in which institutions serving the mentally ill and the mentally retarded go about stripping away from the residents their human dignity, their identity, their motivation, their privacy, their basic human rights. He got the evidence from his own institutions. He has not resigned. But he has clearly identified the evils he wants to fight. And unless *you* clearly identify the things that need to be changed in California, you cannot really expect change to occur. Pointing them out does not have to be accompanied by blaming individuals. I say this over and over again. Because what we are addressing ourselves to are conditions which by far precede the individuals now in office....

Chapter 18
A Society Without Institutions?

*Excerpts from a presentation at the Residential Alternatives Symposium,
University of Hartford, Hartford, CT, December 1979*

Some of you may know that in the state of Massachusetts some years ago, in an admittedly radical move,… we closed almost overnight the several institutions for juvenile delinquents the Commonwealth of Massachusetts had been maintaining. We certainly have not solved thereby the problem of juvenile delinquency, but neither have the people who opposed the closing been able to prove that the closing has worsened our situation in comparison with other states.…

The next example I give is even more interesting and challenging. Throughout the country we had large children's institutions, often known as children's villages or children's homes, and often maintained by religious organizations. Toward the middle of this century, a development took place in our country which substituted a system of foster homes for these institutions. Society had found a better, more timely, answer: Foster homes were the order of the day. But now in the late 1970s, we find at the highest national level, congressional committees have joined social action groups to raise serious questions about the adequacy and appropriateness of the foster care system, advocating *not* a return to the institution, but a much greater reliance on the natural family (in full recognition that these families will need supportive services, including financial support), and for those youngsters where this is not possible, an aggressive program of finding adoptive homes. It should be worth noting…that in sharp contrast to previously held professional opinions, we now have established that we can find good adoptive homes also for children with severe physical and mental handicaps.

…What do we mean by the word *institution?* Sociologists and political scientists use the expression very broadly when they speak of societal institutions such as the family or the community hospital, the day care center. For them a group home serving six young adults in a house on a residential street is an institution.… What your neighbors may see as a nice, family-style home for six young adults is in reality a social institution required to be incorporated with a board of directors, staffing ratios, subject to the jurisdiction of the federal Wage and Hour Administration and subject also to licensing and approval or inspection of several different local and state authorities. (And may I say here in parenthesis that I view with great concern the regulatory orgy one can observe in our field in many states, including my own.)

So, ladies and gentlemen, my answer to the question posed by your program committee is that our society, or one similar to it, cannot function without institutions. But societal institutions are forever subject to change; just look at the best known institution of our society, the public school, and see how its image, structure, and function have been changing during the past century, both internally and externally. And we in New England know that some institutions come to the point where they are no longer effective at all and where the change imposed results in termination.

But of course I realize that your particular focus of interest today is with a particular type of institution, the large, multipurpose, segregated mental retardation institution. Here my answer to you must be blunt. Whether it is called a state school, a regional center, a training school, or a developmental center, the mental retardation institution typically developed in our country in practically every state over the past 100 years is dead.

The decay of Hansfield and Southbury is as noticeable as the decay of Willowbrook, Letchworth Village, and the venerable Fernald School in Massachusetts. The stench of decay may vary, as will the length of time before final collapse. Further generations will look upon them as we today look upon the almshouses and poor farms of the past, a societal institution that at one time performed essential services in ways which became obsolete in the course of time, with a result that what was once a positive contribution became a damaging entity no longer needed.

My own work in the field of mental retardation reflects well the move toward decay of the mental retardation institution. I started out at Letchworth Village in New York State in 1930, when there were dormitories with a hundred beds and 125 children in the beds. Shortly thereafter, as child welfare director for the state of Michigan, I watched with great interest Connecticut's courageous challenge to vested psychiatric interests by calling on the director of a children's home in Illinois to build and administer a new type of institution, the Southbury Training School. However, in general, the 1940s and early 50s saw little change in American mental retardation institutions aside from a steadily increasing crowding and a consequent steady decline in standards of care and in the physical accommodations.

Still, with the new impetus that came from the early beginnings of the parent movement and their demands for justice for their children, we could see some exciting new developments in some of the institutions. I well remember my excitement when, in 1959 in the eastern part of the state of Washington, I visited an institution which not only did superb work in physical habilitation of severely multiply handicapped children but, in a fashion I had never before encountered anywhere, treated these young children as individuals—carefully attending to their personal clothes (even if they were in cribs), referring to each child by his proper name, and involving the entire staff, including secretaries, gardeners, cooks, and drivers, in having a program of individualized one-to-one attention. Somewhat later in a relatively obscure institution in a small state on the Atlantic coast, I found that young, well-trained nurses had learned to teach most severely handicapped children to suck and swallow and even chew. So here was an institution without the usual back wards full of tube-fed children. Later I was involved in designing a new type of institutional facility in Illinois for children classified as moderately and severely retarded, planned with free-standing houses for eight children, sleeping two to a bedroom, and for these four bedrooms there were two regular bathrooms such as one would find in any family home. And there was a kitchen fully equipped to prepare food and a living and a dining room.

Let me admit, it only slowly dawned on me that if these children could live in this type of home, why have 50 of these houses all in one place—away from the community? Why not have these houses distributed throughout this and neighboring communities? And this same question presented itself a little later and even more forcefully when, of all places, in Nampa, Idaho, a pediatrician who served as superintendent of their state institution persuaded the legislature to let him buy six prefabricated houses such as those a local contractor was using in subdivision development. The superintendent had previously invited me and others to consult with him on building plans, but none of us had the imagination to suggest what he actually did. Again the next question was: Why put the buildings on the institution grounds? Why not construct them elsewhere in the community?

Then came other advances—new teaching techniques, the unfolding of behavior modification approaches, and thereby a successful coping with behavior which had previously been determined as unmanageable in the community and requiring institutional care.... With the 1975 enactment of Public Law 94-142, the federal Education of All Handicapped Children Act, another major past reason for institutional care, namely, unavailability of full and appropriate school programs in the community, is being removed....

There is another aspect to this consideration which must be told, and which I am perhaps well prepared to tell, because of my involvement in so many lawsuits in federal and state courts when we deal not with rumor but with sworn testimony, subject to cross examination. Since so many parents express fear of what might happen to their children if they were to go from the institution to live in the community (and I hope I have made it perfectly clear how much I sympathize with these parents and how strong a commitment I feel to deal positively with their concerns), it needs to be said, clearly and unequivocally, that there are vastly greater dangers to their children's physical and mental health and well-being within institutions. It is no accident that we are going to have, early in 1979, a congressional investigation into the problem of abuse of residents in institutions. More children and young people with mental retardation are raped and subject to brutal physical abuse and gross neglect in institutions than in the community. This does not just refer to antiquated institutions with deteriorating physical accommodations. For example, Michigan opened a new institution as a show place around 1960 with an unusually rich complement of outstanding professional staff. So much gross physical and mental abuse occurred over the past several years (not months, but years!) that not only the superintendent but also the director of the state department got their walking papers.

Enough has been said already during this conference about the rapidly escalating cost of institutional care and institutional construction to indicate that this is another point where traditional institutional care has become outdated.

But what do we have instead?... I agree strongly that deinstitutionalization is essentially a negative wrong-way approach. Already in 1973 I testified as follows before the Sub-Committee on Children and Youth of the Senate Committee on Labor and Public Welfare, chaired by then Senator Mondale:

> Too many of the present State efforts towards de-institutionalization have focused only on providing a substitute abode for the person to be moved out of the institution, with often grossly insufficient attention to the many other life-needs of disabled persons. Thus parents and professional workers alike have complained that in many instances the person is merely moved from one large institution to a smaller one, is left without adequate activity, guidance or supervision, still in relative isolation from the rest of the community. There is more than ample evidence that many individuals go to institutions in the first place because of the lack of community programs and

services. Waiting lists for institutions are to a considerable extent waiting lists for a reasonable array of services the community or state has failed to provide.

Therefore, if de-institutionalization is to embrace both prevention of institutionalization and return to the community of individuals now in the institution, it is contingent on the establishment of a network of community services.

Over the years my wife and I have been able to observe how effectively parents can cope even with severe and profound mental retardation if the community provides proper support services, and a great deal has been learned in recent years as to how to provide such services more effectively.

Obviously not all children can always live with their families, whether they are retarded or not retarded, and so we can and will develop in the community an array of services to meet the individual needs of such children *and* adults. All of this is no longer a matter of theoretical projections or wishful thinking, but reflects practical experience.

I feel extremely optimistic about these developments, and yet we cannot afford to ignore what is becoming more and more crystallized as the opposition. It is good that one of your speakers yesterday called to your attention the efforts of some individuals who, strangely, come from the field of ethics and religion and in all seriousness try to deny the humanhood of persons with severe and profound mental retardation. I think we need to be more concerned about individuals who give intelligence (and conversely, limited intelligence) an all-pervasive valuation in terms of human life…. Those of you who have had the privilege of meeting emancipated mentally retarded individuals in the community know what valuable contributions they can make to human life. It is precisely our acquaintance with such mentally retarded individuals in many countries around the world that has given my wife and me so strong and so positive a motivation.

However, there are those professional workers and researchers who will claim that they know that most of the persons presently in our state institutions are so defective as to be incapable of profiting from any training. In other words, under the guise of desiring to afford protection to individuals with severe and profound mental retardation, these colleagues of mine indulge in wholesale denial not just of these persons' human rights, but in essence deny them a human existence.

Proudly pointing to their research findings, they will insist that they can determine who can adjust in the community and who cannot and consequently needs to be institutionalized. But when you look at their research, there seems to be little viable connection between the data being gathered and the actual situations that persons with mental retardation are facing in the community.

There is of course a striking parallel in all of this: In the 1950s and early 60s, research workers in special education and psychology wrote volumes to prove that children who had received an IQ of less than 50 were ineducable and, as such, ineligible for schooling. Yet today these so-called ineducable children go to school and progress in acquiring life skills.

Why my learned colleagues have this urge to downgrade and constrain persons with mental retardation, I do not know, but I am reminded of a paragraph in the foreword my wife and I wrote for a book…entitled *Coming Back: The Community Experiences of*

Deinstitutionalized Mentally Retarded People by Gollay, Freedman, Wyngaarden, and Kurtz. Let me close by quoting this introductory paragraph from our foreword:

> This book brings to the reader a new and important aspect of mental retardation as a social phenomenon. It documents in engaging detail how those traditionally referred to as mentally retarded are steadily advancing toward a more meaningful participation in society, while those who caused them to be known as retarded continue to reflect a "retarded" prejudicial perception. (p. xvii)

PART 6

ADULT CITIZENS IN THE COMMUNITY

Editors' Introduction to Part 6

In this section Dr. Dybwad's words describe the long struggle of people with retardation to be members of the community, not just in the community. For many years well-meaning bureaucrats stood in the way of this goal with a misunderstood need to protect the privacy of people with retardation. They were treated as nonpeople; their eyes were blacked out in pictures, for example. Leaders in the field validated this treatment, and in Dr. Dybwad's view, it was a phenomenal error.

By the 1960s it became clear not only that children with retardation grew up to be adults with retardation, but that they had rights as adults. In a speech at the Woods School in 1960, Dr. Dybwad put forth what was at the time the rather startling notion that the person, as an individual, should be the focus of services. The goal of services should be on the person's assumption of a real and valued role in society. It has taken years for the service system to come to grips with this concept, and its full realization lies in the future.

These speeches and excerpts present and defend the view that there is a real place in society for people with retardation; they describe examples of valued roles that are successfully held by people with retardation: employee, friend, family member, and citizen.

CHAPTER 19
THE MENTALLY RETARDED ADULT'S PLACE IN SOCIETY

Excerpts from a presentation at the 14th International Conference on Social Welfare, Helsinki, Finland, August 1968

John is 21 years of age and is moderately retarded. On a measured intelligence test, this fellow scores an IQ of 40 to 45 but, in addition (and this is very important), he rates fairly well on a social scale. We have not as yet had brains enough to develop adequate quantitative measurements of social adaptation, but we can all make an approximation. While we can express measured intelligence in exact terms, for social adaptation we can only use descriptive and approximate terms, but I want to emphasize that John, with his measured intelligence of 40 to 45 (he tested one way one day and a little differently another day), in his range has a fairly satisfactory standard of social adaptation—he is in good shape. He lives at home with his parents, has the run of the neighborhood, and can do some traveling. Although handicapped, he is capable of using the streetcar or bus to visit a relative; he can make some small purchases in the neighborhood. He went to school, to what the English call a junior training center for the SSN (severely subnormal), or what some call a training class in the United States; it would be a class "on the trainable level." In any case, John went to a place where he had instruction on a regular basis every school day by an instructor who may or may not have been called a "teacher" and who, depending on the country where John lived, may have been paid by the education authorities, the welfare authorities, or the health authorities, but who, nevertheless, worked as a teacher or an instructor. So, as far as I am concerned, John had gone to school. After he completed his schooling, he had some work training. Subsequently he went to a sheltered workshop, where he was engaged in productive activity and was able to move up to work with machines. There he is right now....

...John is technically an adult: He grew to 21 years of age, and then suddenly both his parents are killed in a motor accident. So here he is—21 years of age, moderately mentally retarded, in good health, able to travel and move about in his community. He has his own room and goes by himself each day to the workshop, but now the world breaks down for him because of his parents' death. What are John's needs now as a mentally retarded adult? Where is his place in society? First of all, very obviously, John needs a bed: This is the thing that has definitely been taken away from him at the moment. Due to the parents' death, his home has been dissolved, and in modern society brothers and sisters are no longer around the corner. John is alone. He needs a bed, and he needs a bed in some place, and here we come to a very important part of some of those basic rights we were talking about. John, of course, has a right to choose a place to live. You know this statement could be ridiculed; the point we are making here is, of course, that there are both positive and negative choices, and I think John would most definitely be against being placed somewhere where he has never been. John has a right to choose to remain in the neighborhood where he has always been, where he is known and where people know him, where he is accepted, where the police do not pick him up because he looks strange or suspicious or what not. Yet, as you know, in many countries we felt perfectly comfortable, before we began to think about the rights of the mentally retarded, to take John, in our feeling of great benevolence, to a beautiful new place, specially built, beautifully furnished, 120 miles away, where he has never been. We thought we were just doing fine, we were just doing wonders for John. But why should he have to leave his home community? Here is where this new concept comes to life—his right to choose a place to live. Look at this negatively: Nobody has a right, because of bureaucratic convenience, to shift him suddenly to another place.

Obviously John needs more than merely a bed; it should be a bed in an appropriate social surrounding. I think that John should have the right, now that nobody can replace his parents, to live with some people with whom he can feel congenial. So we would hope that it could be in some kind of hostel in the community where he would be with a few other people of his ability and interests, and could live in a situation where his room should approximate that kind of place where he lived before....

Now, since John is deprived of his family, one right we should give him is that he should have some way to express his identity. Perhaps the most basic of John's rights is to be John—John Smith, John Larson, John Sterner. Whoever he is, he is a person, and he should have a right to express this by putting some pictures on the wall. We have gone through literally dozens of hostels, well-furnished, even expensively furnished, with not a place for personal belongings, not a picture, and everything polished like in a furniture exhibit. So there is reason to emphasize that he has a right to express himself.

Next, of course, John needs to have someone to look after him. His parents used to look after him; they guided and counseled him. Who will do this now? In the Netherlands they have a new type of professional person for this who is called a social pedagogue. This is a very interesting combination of terms, and it does not mean a legal guardian. In some countries it may be possible to combine these two functions, gaining some advantages; on the other hand, this may be difficult. Basically what John needs is somebody to stand by him when he has small problems or large ones, to help him, for example, arrange trips and so on, perhaps a visit to the brother who lives in the country.

John, of course, can no longer depend on the financial security given to him by his parents. He has a job in a sheltered workshop where, obviously, he cannot earn adequately enough (unless it would be a most exceptional workshop), but certainly he has a right to be paid properly for his work. Even so, he needs financial assistance in some way to make up the difference between what he earns in the sheltered workshop and what it costs him to live. This would be in the form of a pension or some other form of disability payments. In any case, John now needs, and we must provide for him, a different financial security, and I think what should be stressed here is that this should come to him as his own income, from which deductions are made for his board and maintenance. But we should not assume the right to take care of this without consulting John, just giving him some pocket money every week. No, he has a right to receive money and to participate to the level of his ability in these financial transactions. Time and again, we have been surprised how much even some quite handicapped young adults are aware of money and take pleasure in saving.

The next point is that while John lived with his parents, he perhaps did not feel quite so much need for social contacts, but now he most definitely needs such contacts, with persons of his own age and older and with members of the other sex. How can we provide this for him? It is important to emphasize that these contacts must be age-appropriate. John is no longer a child; he does not want to live with children; he wants to live as an adult in some kind of adult setting. John should also expect from us that we maintain his former life pattern as much as possible, including maintaining his family ties, what little they may be. John has a right, of course, to recreational activities, and it has also increasingly been our experience with those young people of post-school-age who are in a stimulating work situation that they should have a right to adult education. It may sound strange to some of you at first, yet in several countries there are now in existence—and adult retardates are utilizing—special learning opportunities, coming to them *as adults*.

John has a job, and we must of course try to select for him a living place so he can commute if at all possible. Yet we should not make all life easy and provide him with living quarters next door to or in the same house with a workshop in order to cut down his (and that means our) problems. I think this right to normal living, the "right to normalization," to quote the Danish and Swedish philosophy, certainly includes the right to commute between work and home.

And now I come to the final question, which we cannot fully answer here although I wish we had adequate time to discuss it. After we have provided all of these things for John—he is in a sheltered workshop where he is a good worker, he no longer lives with his parents but in a nice hostel—one day he comes to us and says, "I want to marry Louise." Then what? First of all, we should talk with John in social terms about how he thinks he would manage this: Where would he live, how would he pay the rent, who would cook, and so on? But suppose John is more persistent than we might give him credit for, and he meets our arguments step by step.

At that point we are forced to admit to ourselves (though few would have the courage to explain it to John, too) that what concerns us far more than the cooking and the rent is the fear we have about sexual involvement and specifically about procreation. But is our fear justified? Should we not first of all find out whether one or both of these young people might not be sterile? If no, should we not make available to them modern methods of pregnancy prevention?

So if we feel that John and Louise can manage their domestic affairs in some fashion, why should they not be married and live together? Can we not develop, as we have in some modern facilities for the aged, simple small apartments in a larger housing complex, with somebody looking after the welfare of those there? Might this be an answer?

I have prescribed for you a few of the concrete problems which will face us when we begin to apply broad philosophical statements under the topic "The Mentally Retarded Adult's Place in Society" to the specific situation of one individual. May I, in parentheses, make one other comment which is not in accordance with my story, for which I presumed that John's parents died suddenly. More and more often, some thoughtful people wonder whether it would not be much better for John and for his parents if a place for him could be selected before the parents died, so that John can begin to live a life in a hostel or small group home while the parents are still alive, and he can still visit back and forth, and they can help him to adjust to this new life. Would this not be much better than waiting until tragedy strikes, forcing John, at the psychologically worst possible moment, to adjust to a totally new life?…

…This will help you to see more clearly what we need to do in order to guarantee for the mentally retarded all those individual rights which they are capable of exercising to their own benefit and without undue harm to the community, and which will gain for them personal dignity and a place as adults in society.

Chapter 20
International Developments in the Social Rehabilitation of the Handicapped

Excerpt from a public lecture at the University of British Columbia, Vancouver, January 1976

No matter what definition is used, *normalization* is suspect, no doubt about it; in any gathering of persons concerned with rehabilitation and other human services, the mere mention of the term will produce argumentation and raised blood pressure, particularly on the part of those concerned with physical disability.

This represents a most peculiar switch: Undeniably in the past, there has been a distinct unwillingness on the part of organizations dealing with physical disability to become involved with mental retardation, because it was felt that mentally retarded people deviated so far from the normal that it would distort and damage the public image of physical disability to be identified with mental retardation.

But now when from within the field of mental retardation, as one product of a veritable avalanche of progress and change, there comes the normalization principle, some of the same sources from the physical disabilities field insist almost indignantly that normalization is not for us; it is inappropriate and unrealistic for persons with physical disability.

I shall not attempt within the framework of my presentation to present a detailed account of the philosophical base and rationale for the concept of normalization. Let me just point out that the origin of the effort to introduce the concept of normalization was the realization that a specific strategy had to be developed to counteract the process of denormalization which over the past 75 years made such deep inroads into society's dealing with handicapped individuals such as persons with epilepsy, mental retardation, cerebral palsy, and a host of other disabilities and, in particular, persons with multiple disabilities. In other words, normalization is a rational attempt to deal with the very conditions which have tended to deepen and reinforce prejudice and tended to set the severely handicapped apart from the rest of society.

Even maximum normalization does not remove all problems, does not create an Elysian trouble-free life for the handicapped person. To the contrary, as my use of the word *Elysian* indicates, only in mythology does one meet up with a state of complete happiness. Normal on our earth is trouble and strife, trial and tribulation, and the handicapped person has the right of being exposed to it. Normalization includes the dignity of risk, a concept Robert Perske (1972) brought back from a visit to Denmark and Sweden a few years ago.

Social psychologists have long ago discovered that a very useful approach to avoidance is to misunderstand and misapply a concept, and this is what one can observe here. Normalization does not refer to something that is done *to* people; I certainly do not want to "normalize" another human being. Normalization refers to facilities and services, to situations; indeed to the life situation—of a person. It responds to the past (and unfortunately still present) process of *de*-normalization by trying to reestablish a normal equilibrium.

But why do we encounter so often from parents, from the staff of agencies, and even from some disabled persons such vehement objection to the concept of normalization? Because, I dare say, these individuals have made extensive accommodation to the processes of denormalization, dehumanization, and segregation and now exhibit the all-too-familiar resistance to a pattern of change that inevitably will bring along conflict and necessitate special effort.

Of course this type of change has occurred before. In the field of epilepsy, the process of normalization (though not under that name) has made slow but steady progress over the past decades, and this has happened to an even more pronounced degree in the field of blindness. Indeed, if you have at all questions about my referring to the resistance to normalization on the part of the staffs of agencies, study the fierce struggle two decades or so ago between the agencies and associations *for* the blind and the emerging associations *of* the blind.

In essence, then, normalization is an effort to effect new and more appropriate *patterns of living* for handicapped persons and in particular for those with multiple handicaps.

One very striking example of efforts to normalize the environment for handicapped people is the very forceful international campaign toward "freedom of access." As one travels about in Europe, in the Americas, and even on some of the other continents, one is confronted increasingly with the stylized wheelchair picture indicating that this particular building has no barriers to free access and allows persons in wheelchairs and with other physical impediments to enter, to travel to upper stories, to use toilets, etc. etc.

I realize that opinions differ sharply when it comes to ways of educating the public, but in my opinion freedom-of-access signs will become a powerful reminder to the general public to think about their handicapped fellow citizens, and this should not just apply to the orthopedically handicapped or other nonambulant persons, but should affect public attitudes toward all handicapped persons.

"Freedom of access" leads us logically to the problem of housing. Even well-informed, well-motivated colleagues frequently raise the question: "To what extent can severely multihandicapped persons live among us?" Let me state for myself that to me there is no limit to that if "among us" refers to the community where we live. Quite specifically, for example, I have always maintained that there is no reason why the most severely handicapped persons presently bedridden in large dormitories in institutions could not get very adequate care in specialized facilities right in the community, preferably not too far from a hospital, provided, of course, that the citizens have seen to it that the appropriate regulations provide not only for the technical aspects of adequate care but also for a basic human environment in such a facility.

Will this really bring about good integration? Well, to this I would raise the counterquestion: Does social integration work out well anywhere for the full range of a *non*handicapped population? Why should we demand or expect from the handicapped persons what we have not achieved for the general population?

Of the essence in our residential planning must be *continuum,* a wide range of domiciliary provisions from the single apartment—not tied to *any* service or supervisory pattern—to the semimedical facility providing a program of rehabilitative nursing, with an almost limitless list of other types of domiciliary provisions.

Here again *normalization* is the watchword. Why should any disabled person have to sleep in an unattractive but expensive hospital bed when he can safely sleep in a much cheaper simple wooden one that can serve as an attractive sofa during the day? It was during a visit I made many years ago to a small Swedish facility for persons with cerebral palsy that this was forcefully brought home to me.

There is no reason why people cannot eat in small groups even in a large nursing care facility, why one should not be able to lock one's room as long as a master key is available for emergencies. Nurse's stations are still being designed by architects (upon urging from the administration), even though the normal activities typical of such a station are not practiced in a small facility and their presence creates an overwhelming institutional atmosphere.

It might be said that in no area have we denormalized and dehumanized the severely physically disabled person as much as in the sphere of their sexual life. At long last this has not just been recognized as a crucial problem, but some effective action is being taken. Perhaps some of you have already seen the film *Like Other People,* showing a tender relationship developing between two wheelchair-bound people afflicted with cerebral palsy. For me it was a most revealing and most moving experience. I also hope many of you will have an opportunity to read *A Right to Love,* a report on public and professional attitudes toward the sexual and emotional needs of handicapped people, by Ann Shearer, one of England's most gifted social journalists and cofounder of the Campaign for the Mentally Handicapped. What it brought to my mind was an equally moving vision of the days of Martin Luther King, when black men marched through the streets of American cities holding up a sign proclaiming "I am a man!" Is it not also an aspect of normalization that we shall no longer abrogate the rights of severely multiply handicapped persons to proclaim and experience the fact I AM A MAN, I AM A WOMAN? Thus, it is gratifying to find now in the professional literature serious discussion with regard to the specific aid we need to give the most severely physically handicapped to achieve a modicum of sexual satisfaction.

I purposely have mentioned this area of sexual concern and activity because it is a good place to test our own feelings toward the handicapped person. Before we start checking up on how far others have gone in giving the multiply handicapped adult his due, we ourselves must check how far we have succeeded and how far we still have to go in according him his individuality, his dignity, his right to be heard, his right to make decisions affecting him, his right *to be a person.*...

Chapter 21
Normalization and Integration— Shifting Empires

Excerpts from Working Paper presented at the Symposium on Normalization and Integration, organized for the International League of Societies for the Mentally Handicapped by the National Association for Retarded Citizens, USA, Airlie, VA, August 1976

Over the last years the mere mention of the term *normalization* has been sure to bring out critical comments and argumentation. Controversy develops around potent issues, and the potency of the normalization principle is implied in the formulation of the topic for this session, which links this new concept to the shifting of empires....

It was not surprising that the first official mention of normalization as a principle guiding public policy did not occur until 1959, when Denmark enacted a statute which radically changed its predominantly residential care system for mentally retarded persons. This legislation indeed did some very specific "empire shifting" of such great significance that it deserved to take first place in the listing of specific examples I would like to offer as a basis for further discussion.

Nine Exemplary Shifts

1. From a medical monopoly to a (at times dubious) sharing with education, rehabilitation, and social services.

Any critical comments about the medical domination of our care systems for mentally retarded persons needs to be preceded by an acknowledgment that it was largely the physicians who first became interested in developing educational and rehabilitation programs for mentally retarded persons. However, as has been amply documented, as time progressed, the medical care as much as education and rehabilitation became less and less adequate and the asylum aspect (often referred to as custodial care) came more and more to the fore until, at least in some countries, the lack of rehabilitative medicine in the institutions, and in the community as well, became a scandal.

In Denmark medical superintendents were replaced by a four-man directorate (administrator, physician, educator, social service director). The theme repeated itself in many variations in all industrial countries. It is worthy of note that most recently, in line with a very considerable strengthening of public health forces (i.e., a broader base than merely the practicing physician), one can observe in the United States a shift back toward greater attention to health requirements. There is a reassertion that education and rehabilitation must take second place to the presumably more basic public health concerns. In part this is due to an interesting phenomenon. Greater interest on the part of the public (and in particular on the part of the present associations for the retarded) in achieving and safeguarding better standards in day and residential services and facilities for retarded individuals have brought about a demand for standards so that the providers of service, whether public or private, can be held accountable. The motivation for such demands for accountability stems from the same concerns as the normalization principle.

However, a strange paradox makes its appearance. Standards are readily expressed in concise language when they pertain to basic health protection, hygiene, and fire and building safety. On the other hand, vital concerns such as safeguarding privacy, personal dignity, right to participate in decision making, the dignity of risk, do not lend themselves to precise regulatory enforcement. Consequently this demand for standards, for accountability, has resulted at least in part in bringing back an overemphasis on health and safety as compared with more humanistic concerns supporting the developmental growth of the individual resident within a framework of normalization.

It is important to stress that we cannot simply talk about a line-up of education, rehabilitation, and social service against the physicians. Rather, there is very considerable struggle for power going on in a number of countries between these nonmedical fields. The reason for this is fairly clear. Professional roles as between the various professions tend to overlap increasingly. Functions that are carried on by the health department in one country are done by education in another country, in a third by social service. Where formerly it had been impossible to interest any public agency to initiate programs for mentally retarded persons, one may now observe competitiveness between the departments. What once was no man's land has become disputed territory. Obviously this puts consumer advocacy groups in a strategically favorable position.

2. From the institution as dominating, "rich" focal point to the institution as one part of a network of community resources.

Here we see perhaps the "shifting empire" in its most dramatic form. In quite a number of the industrial countries, an increasing tendency to segregate mentally retarded persons caused institutions to grow into large cumbersome entities with thousands of residents and thousands of employees. Superintendents had a great deal of power, and until approximately World War II the superintendent's power was exercised also over the employees, many of whom lived in barracks-like buildings on the grounds of the institution. "Progressive" superintendents pioneered in carrying at least some of the services closer to the community. Many superintendents came to see the institution as the focal point also for information and expertise in mental retardation and were loath to accept the developing mental retardation competence in community agencies.

Sociologists have long shown that system maintenance (or in American slang "defending your turf") is a powerful inhibitor of change, and the journals are full of articles demonstrating just that. Since the normalization principle is quite correctly assumed to have been one of the principal motivating factors toward lessened dependence on institutional care, those who wish to defend the institution attack the normalization principle as an unrealistic concept. The intensity with which the institutional empire is being defended was highlighted recently in the United States, where a superintendent joined with the employee's union representative and other staff members in purchasing advertising space in the local newspaper warning the citizens about the threat to their interest as home-owners if plans for closing the institution and moving residents into the community would be realized.

Actually, the institutional empires are shifting only slowly, even in Sweden and Denmark, where the significant change has not been a marked decrease in institutional beds but rather a rapid growth of community services.

3. From centralized governmental control to decentralized decision making.

The normalization principle is geared to the individual human being and his need for growth and support. Hence a system that is guided by the normalization principle is a system where service delivery at the right time and the right place under the right circumstances becomes a focal concern, a system where there will be less insistence on the bureaucratic process and more emphasis on human values.

It should be stressed that there are, of course, other reasons why decentralization may be introduced in a governmental structure, but normalization policies cannot be well effected without it, and it thus becomes a threat to those clearly in favor of strong centralized impersonal bureaucracy. In this battle of shifting empires, centralized government will feel more comfortable with large, authoritarian institutions than with decentralized, individualized, dispersed community services.

4. From a closed, academic exclusive school system to a system of open inclusive schools teaching basic human life skills.

Normalization has been recognized in the realm of the public school in North America by use of expression *mainstreaming*. Mainstreaming stands for an open school system in which the needs of handicapped pupils are met in an environment and program which are as close as possible to that of the average school population.

This does not mean, as is often falsely claimed by opponents of mainstreaming, that there should be no more special classes in the schools. Rather, no one should be in a special class who with assistance can manage in a regular class, and special classes should be as close to regular classes in location, general programming, and management as the special educational needs of the pupils will permit.

Again we are facing different aspects of shifting empires. For the educational traditionalist for whom school was a privilege granted to those deemed worthy, who rationalized his exclusionary policies as a professional responsibility, mainstreaming meant an attack on his authority and integrity. On the other hand, educators who welcome mainstreaming and who saw in it a greatly enlarged opportunity to discharge another conception of professional responsibility, namely, to serve all children no matter how handicapped or how disadvantaged, arrived at a vastly broadened concept of the role of the public school, one that inevitably intruded on what had been the territory of other agencies. To be specific, a "zero reject" program that tries to reach and serve the educational needs of every school-age child no matter how handicapped inevitably will become involved with medical as well as social problems and a broad coordinating role that will be perceived as threatening by the keepers of other professional empires.

5. From vocational rehabilitation to human rehabilitation.

The history of rehabilitation as a structured, governmental activity makes clear that it started as a very narrow vocational program for very specific vocational groups, such as merchant marine men, railroad men, and of course disabled war veterans. Even the so-progressive International Labor Organization Recommendation 99 excluded from rehabilitation those who can *neither* be prepared for, nor have reasonable prospects of, securing and retaining suitable employment. Even more than the public school systems, governmental rehabilitation programs in the industrial countries felt justified to adopt broad exclusionary policies. It remained to the Declaration *on* the Rights of Disabled Persons, adopted by the United Nations General Assembly in December 1975, to set forth that rehabilitation is a right that shall be granted to all disabled persons without any exception whatsoever.

The problems of empire shifting in the vocational area are much like those in the educational area. Conservative rehabilitation agencies, which saw a policy of selection of what they considered "feasible candidates" as a major responsibility, and whose staff is narrowly trained in the vocational area, will resist a new, greatly expanded role which now forces them to work with those whom they formerly identified as incapable of responding to their efforts.

On the other hand, rehabilitation agencies proceeding in the spirit of the new United Nations Declaration on the Rights of Disabled Persons, which firmly embodies the principle of normalization, will quickly come into conflict with existing social or health agencies which in the past have been left to care for the more severely disabled.

6. From charity to rights.

The emergence of the normalization principle had a very decisive effect not only on mentally retarded person but also on their families and in particular their parents. The slogan "from charity to rights" indicates the passing of the benevolent despots. Parents became aware of their children's entitlement and no longer had to beg for favors. Parents also became aware that they had increasingly a right to access information about their children. Those who built and safeguarded professional empires understood well that it is possible to build up one's power by refusing to share information or at least making it difficult to obtain it.

Recently a British psychologist contributed an article to the journal *New Psychiatry* in which she suggested that parents should be given, in writing, a detailed, intelligible summary of their child's assessment. In several of the states in the United States parents now have, either by statute or by regulation, the right to inspect their child's school records.

7. From professional decision making to shared decision making.

The normalizing and dehumanizing practices of the past discriminated against the handicapped person by denying him self-determination and a right to be heard when decisions were made which greatly affected him. In the case of severe handicap and particularly so with mental retardation and cerebral palsy, the parents of the afflicted children were also victims of prejudgment, were described as anxiety-ridden and emotional, and were accused of wishful thinking and of unwillingness to face facts, and hence were frequently excluded from deliberations which vitally affected their child's whole future.

In the wake of normalization and integration and the affirmation of basic personal rights, and under pressure from parent and consumer organizations, procedures are being introduced allowing parents to participate when decisions are made affecting their children. To a lesser extent, but increasingly, the disabled person, even be he a child, is considered entitled to participate in such decisions. In particular there has been recognition that persons who are directors of a service or facility such as an institution or a foster care agency cannot be permitted to make decisions on behalf of the child or adult that have far-reaching consequences, such as sterilization, or elective surgery (i.e., not of an emergency nature).

8. From parental control to recognition of the rights of retarded children.

As previously pointed out, normalization is such a broad concept that it may well trigger seemingly contradictory effects. We have just discussed how parents have gained more rights, more of a voice, but the contrary is also the case. In the past parents were not questioned when they made far-reaching decisions concerning their retarded children. This practice now conflicts with the new assertion that mentally retarded persons are citizens endowed with rights of their own. The conflict is particularly apparent when their child has become an adult. But even in the case of retarded children, there is a growing recognition of the limits of parental power. For example, parents in the past were automatically presumed to have the right to arrange for the life-long institutionalization of their retarded child. This is being strongly contested. There was a time, of course, when the *pater familias*, the father or grandfather, ruled the family with total power, to the point that he could sell his child or otherwise exclude him from the family group. Nowadays parental power in general is far more narrowly circumscribed, with variation from country to country. In the case of the severely handicapped and in particular the mentally retarded child, parental power was assumed to be absolute even to the point of ordering a child born with serious defects to be killed. Now with the principle of normalization and recognition of the handicapped child's own rights as a person and a citizen, parental power individually and collectively has become another "shifting empire"—not be to abolished, to be sure, but to be "normalized" to be more in keeping with parental power in society at large.

9. From parent-sponsored associations as owner or operator of service empires to ARCs as monitor, advocate, communicator, stimulator.

The beginning of the movement of parents of retarded children was characterized by the organization of small cooperative play groups and school classes. Some of the associations have kept on adding services, built and purchased buildings, hired staff to such an extent that their role as consumers has become secondary to that of providers of services. In some instances they have grown to million-dollar enterprises, creating conflicting roles for the membership as between being consumers and service operators....

Effects of the Changing Policies

Certain effects of the new policies of normalization and integration deserve special mention.

1. Courts in the United States have expressed the normalization principle in terms of a right to the least restrictive alternative. The "shifting empire" concept is demonstrated here by a reversal from previously accepted procedure. "Can we release him?" becomes, "May we keep him any longer?" "What special service is appropriate for him?" becomes, "Is there any reason for a special service?" References should be made here to Ed Skarnulis's point that we must move away from the traditional "residential assumption" (1976).

2. The now widely accepted right to treatment has an interesting corollary in the right not to be treated. (A resident in an institution may refuse drug therapy that is not necessary for life preservation.)

3. In general one can observe a shifting in the burden of proof in favor of the handicapped person.

4. As the normalization principle—the assertion of the rights of the retarded person and the new policy of avoidance of institutionalization if less restrictive alternatives should be available—is becoming a reality, we face a challenge of working out new solutions for families having difficulties in coping with their mentally retarded child or adult.

5. The phasing down and ultimate phasing out of the traditional large multipurpose residential institution raises problems not only for the authorities who relied on these facilities to discharge their official functions or for the families who in the past utilized these institutions, but also for the considerable number of employees who have depended on these institutions for their livelihood and for the many small communities for which the institution provided a primary economic stability....

Chapter 22
Normalization and Its Impact on Social and Public Policy

Excerpts from a presentation to a conference of the National Institute on Normalization and Contemporary Practice in Mental Retardation, Estes Park, CO, February 1980

When I first wrote of the normalization principle in 1969 in the first edition of a publication of the President's Committee on Mental Retardation, I linked it with human management programming (Dybwad, 1969a). I have come to recognize that a considerable part of the vehement and persistent opposition to the normalization principle coming from professional colleagues derives from the misunderstanding that the normalization principle implies a normative activity (i.e., someone is being normalized), and I realize that my use of the term *human management* was unfortunate. It implies a conceptualization of human interaction I can no longer accept. There is an obvious and vital difference between the terms *making available* on the one hand and *establishing and maintaining* on the other, and, as I shall indicate later, much of the opposition to the normalization principle focuses on this factor.

A great deal has been written by those who oppose or question the normalization principle because of its origin in another culture (i.e., the Scandinavian countries) with a cultural orientation which is presumed to be quite different from ours. A review of the historical facts evokes a slightly different interpretation. The normalization principle was first enunciated in Denmark in 1958 by Niels-Erik Bank-Mikkelsen, who had been commissioned to carry through an administrative reform brought about by strong advocacy from the newly organized movement of parents of children with mental handicaps. As Mr. Bank-Mikkelsen has since stated (1976), the basis for his policy of normalization was the need for clear and vigorous action to terminate the shocking denormalizing conditions he found in the traditional Danish mental retardation residential institutions. In other words, as first conceived, normalization was a specific strategy to counteract the process of denormalization in institutions.

Insufficient attention has been paid by American critics of the normalization principle to a striking parallel in our own country. David Vail, as director of mental health and retardation institutions in Minnesota, published a book entitled *Dehumanization and the Institutional Career* (1966), a very detailed critique of the day-to-day practices in the institutions under his care. Unfortunately, unlike Bank-Mikkelsen, he did not spell out a corresponding corrective program of humanization in the first book, and his untimely death deprived us of further writings. But in his book there is a section entitled "The Round of Life" which is strikingly similar to Bengt Nirje's (1969) "normal routine of life"; in a subsequent section, David Vail discusses the need for a normal rhythm of the day and the need for normal arrangements for eating. In other words, what we can observe here are the reactions of two administrators concerned about similar phenomena inherent in traditional institutional practices, one in Denmark and the other in the United States.

I was also struck by the comment in the introductory prospectus prepared by the Conference staff, that the normalization principle "may have lessened both the need and respect for parental opinion and involvement." As far as I have been able to determine, the first printed reference in the United States to the normalization principle in mental retardation appeared in October 1961, in the newsletter of the Saginaw County Association for Retarded Children in Michigan. Betty Hansen, the association's president, in an editorial entitled "Let Them Be Normal," urged other parents not to deprive their children of the opportunity to attend school like other children (in those days, of course, a segregated school, but at least a school). "Sometimes we parents with handicapped children become so absorbed in the differences in them, that we forget that they are as normal as any child in so many ways." Her editorial closes with these words: "But if we are to do our best as parents of our retarded child, we maybe should be prepared to let him be as normal as he is. The child attending a training center is being given just this opportunity."

The National Association for Retarded Children, which a year earlier at its annual convention raised the question, "Are We Retarding the Retarded?" (Dybwad, 1964a), reprinted and widely distributed Mrs. Hansen's editorial.

This comment does not seek to imply that the normalization principle has been generally accepted by parents. Here again, it is normal to be different, and we deal (as in the professional field) with a broad spectrum of opinion. Still, it is significant that it was a parent and president of a local parents' association who first enunciated the importance of normal environments and experiences, 8 years before Bengt Nirje's (1969) chapter in *Changing Patterns* was first presented to the professional community....

Normalization and Community Integration

The impact of normalization on the public at large is an area where there seems to be the greatest difference of opinion. Professional literature and conferences like this seem to dwell on the need to educate the public toward better understanding of and tolerance for persons with mental retardation, lest open hostility and contempt bring harm to these defenseless individuals. I take a quite contrary view. As one who has been active in this field for 41 years, I have been amazed and gratified how well the general public has responded to the increasing visibility of persons even with substantial degrees of retardation. Considering the vast numbers of such people who are now walking our streets, shopping in supermarkets, who use buses and trolley cars, attend ball games, travel by plane or subway, and occupy neighborhood homes, the infrequency of untoward incidents is astonishing. To be sure, there has been much outcry when a group home for retarded persons is to be established in a residential zone, but a nursery school would draw heavy opposition just as well. What is significant and to be observed with great frequency, indeed in the vast majority of cases, is that once the home is established, the prior protest notwithstanding, the opposition fades away.

This brings me to a criterion often used to judge the success of normalization programs, which is the extent of integration into the new neighborhood. That is a difficult matter, not just for persons with special needs, but for many of us. I personally do not even recall the names of all our neighbors in the one-family-home neighborhood in our small town where we have lived for 12 years. Our social contacts are elsewhere. Integration into a neighborhood is not easily achieved, indeed. But that certainly does not suggest that we should accept social isolation, and most of the group homes I have visited in various states seem to have established some outreach to neighbors and other meaningful community contacts. To repeat, I have not seen any study of consequence that has accumulated factual data of large-scale specific acts of hostility toward retarded persons to back up the oft-repeated stories of community rejection. If you have documented quantified data, I should be most interested to review this information.

What is of concern to me, however, is the increasingly noticeable rejection by professional workers of normalization activities which enable persons with a substantial degree of mental retardation to live in the community. I have been sufficiently concerned about this development to suggest to some of my colleagues in psychology departments that they should try to stimulate some of their doctoral students to study in-depth the phenomenon of this professional rejection. What is it that causes well-trained professional workers of recognized standing to become irritated when they are told of success stories among persons with severe and profound mental retardation?

It is the professional groups, not the folks in the neighborhood, not the man on the street, who will have an influence on public and social policy. Yet many of them have a minimum of meaningful contact with the persons about whom they are ready to make exclusionary and restrictive decisions based on unsubstantiated assumptions related to irrelevant data. I am keenly aware of the provocative nature of this statement, but it needs to be said, and I hope our discussions will touch on this problematic area....

There are increasing instances when newspaper stories report in responsible and respectful ways about events involving mental retardation. Perhaps some of you will understand how touched I was when I read recently in the *Boston Globe* a fairly lengthy obituary about a young woman who had died as a result of injuries suffered in an automobile accident a year earlier. There was a reference to the fact that she had graduated from a school I recognized as one of the old special schools, and there was also reference to her having worked in a place I knew as a sheltered workshop. When a young woman with Down's syndrome can die in dignity and have an obituary which extolled her kindness and her popularity, I am bold enough to say that normalization has brought us a long way.

CHAPTER 23
ACCESS TO WORK

Excerpt from a presentation, "The Mentally Retarded in the Changing Society," at the Third Asian Conference on Mental Retardation, Bangalore, India, November 1977

At this point I would like to comment on an interesting and sharp difference of opinion about a change in our society. There are those who feel that any society which becomes industrialized has less and less use for unskilled labor as technology requires higher and more sophisticated job qualifications. In other words, technology is driving the retarded worker out of the labor market. A Puerto Rican psychologist, Carlos Albizu-Miranda (1970), holds the exact opposite view. He insists that there is much confusion between the complication of the industrial society's machines and the complication of its jobs; he maintains, "The more complicated a machine is to put together, the easier it is likely to be to operate. The simplification of the job is the main selling point of machinery manufacturers. Nor are their arguments specious."

I strongly agree with Professor Albizu-Miranda's viewpoints and would go one step further. Even the manufacture of some of society's wondrous machines can be surprisingly simple. I stand in awe before a television set, but in the Netherlands retarded adults with Down syndrome have been engaged in the manufacture of Phillips TV sets for at least 15 years. Nor do I want to limit Albizu-Miranda's argument to the actual work requirements; rather, the changing society is confronting the person of limited ability with rather limited demands. He need not read but can get information from radio or TV. He can shop in a supermarket without uttering a word; he can use public transportation, buy precooked food, and use the telephone instead of writing letters. If he is physically disabled, there are now available a multitude of prosthetic devices, motorized wheelchairs, and special equipment to facilitate the tasks of daily living.

Yet handicapped individuals, and particularly those with mental handicap, have a hard time getting employment. The reason for this does not lie in their inability to work but rather in the unwillingness of employers and workers alike to give them access to work. In other words, we need to differentiate between the changing circumstances in our societal existence, that are favorable to the handicapped (such as technology) and the expressed attitude of society, which is very benign toward the retarded child but competitively rejecting toward the retarded adult in search of employment.

Of course, this problem will make itself felt in Asia much sooner in the areas with a high industrial concentration and an organized (unionized) labor force and will be of little significance in the vast rural areas. But since mental retardation programs also will tend to develop sooner in the industrial areas, this matter cannot be overlooked.

There remains the possibility of yet another solution of this dilemma faced by mentally retarded adults, a solution which so far has been discussed only in the most general terms. The proponents of this solution question the well-established presumption that the goal for each retarded person (at least for the men) should be productive employment. Instead, they envision—rather vaguely—"alternatives to work in the form of functional roles suitable for the disabled and directing efforts toward formulating new and innovative programs in which the measure of success will be in terms of life satisfaction." It remains to be seen whether any country will constructively develop such a solution as a vital societal response or whether this will be a dole-like solution reserved just for persons with severe handicaps, thereby further segregating them into a denormalized situation....

Part 7

Advocacy and Empowerment

Editors' Introduction to Part 7

Advocacy by and with people with retardation is a relatively new idea. While parents have for decades advocated for their children, their goals were usually appropriate services. Families advocated for system changes that would create real opportunities for their sons and daughters to learn, perhaps with other children, and to hold jobs, perhaps with other employees. By working in and against systems in which people with all kinds of disabilities were, *if anything,* service recipients, advocates—both parents and people with disabilities—sought to make the services at least relevant to real lives.

The concept of *empowerment* brings a new dimension to the notion of advocacy. No longer are advocates those who speak for others; today the voice of people with retardation is loud in its demand for power to make decisions, to influence policy, and to advise about practice. No longer are self-advocates looking simply for better services; instead, they seek the chance to play on a level playing field with people who do not have disabilities.

Even so, the service community continues to think about speaking *for* self-advocates. We invite self-advocates to advise the service organization, yet we maintain structures that create subcommittees to advise self-advocates. We continue to maintain a distance between the "providers" of service and the "recipients" of services, and, as a result, the power within the service field remains with providers. As a field, we need to begin to recognize that the present system is not contributing to the empowering of individuals with disabilities; it is actually impeding their empowerment.

We keep people "retarded." We teach, we advise, we help—we actually encourage—second-class citizenship by creating and maintaining distance relationships with people with retardation. We can't imagine that "they" can teach "us." Dr. Dybwad identifies this as "the problem for the future." In these speeches, he points out the many ways in which the service system fosters dependence and considers the roles that are familiar for families and people with disabilities. Dr. Dybwad encouraged and participated in using the courts as an aid to advocacy—the theme of a couple of the speeches in this section. His challenge to the disability field is to reinvent itself so that these old roles can be abandoned and replaced with opportunities for people with disabilities to achieve power over their own lives.

Chapter 24
We Have to Fight

Introductory comments at the International League of Societies for Persons With Mental Handicap Symposium on the Future Role of Voluntary Associations, Madrid, November 1984

My dear friend Victor Wahlstrom has assigned to me as the theme for my introductory comments the topic "We Have to Fight." As I was sitting in my office wondering how I could best start out my remarks, my mind was wandering across the years of my association with the International League of Societies for Persons With Mental Handicap, and suddenly I was back in Nairobi in that imposing conference hall where we had in 1982 our Eighth World Congress. And there they were, that marvelous group of self-advocates, from eight different countries, speaking different languages, facing an audience of 700 people from 70 different countries around the world. Those of you who were there will remember with what clarity they conveyed to us their beliefs, their hopes, their wants, and how effectively they later on answered questions put to them from that international audience. Their concerns, indeed their future, are certainly worth fighting for.

And then my thoughts wandered off in another direction, to a hospital nursery with a newborn infant with Down syndrome who needs routine surgery, but the doctor and the parents have agreed to refuse this child the life-saving surgery, because they think the life of this baby is not worth saving just because of the fact that he has Down syndrome and will be a child with mental handicap. England, Canada, and the United States have freely admitted that these situations occur, and we may well wonder what happens in other countries. Here, I think, we face another fighting issue which deeply reflects a prejudice not just against this infant but against all people with Down syndrome. The League and its member societies will have to fight against these prejudicial attitudes.

That brought to my mind a situation in a nearby city where the city council wants to establish regulations which would make it much more difficult for three or four persons with an intellectual handicap to reside together in an apartment or one-family house, even though they have lived in that city much of their life and hold jobs there. Fighting for the right of people with handicaps to live in the community is certainly a challenge facing all of us. This is what came to my mind, but there are, of course, many other situations equally challenging us to stand up and fight.

So let me bring you this morning this call to arms, together with a declaration of faith, faith in our ability to sustain and widen the progress that has been made in the field of mental handicap over the recent decades, faith in the ever-growing readiness of community and society to accept persons with handicaps, and faith, above all, in the ever-increasing capacity of persons with handicaps and, indeed, with severe mental handicap to find a place in our society. This faith is what brought representatives from 70 nations to Nairobi. This faith brought again to this assembly such wide representation from far distant countries. To this I wish to add as a third point my conviction that the forward thrust of the associations formed by parents and friends of persons with mental handicap has provided a strong base from which we all can carry on a good fight.

Many good and useful thoughts will be expressed here by the various symposium participants regarding a multitude of phenomena in the life of the League's member societies. What I would like to stress is that these organizations reflect *people,* and I hope to strengthen, reaffirm, and undergird your confidence in the League and the work of its member societies by a brief review of the remarkable people who have helped shape its destiny.

There were, of course, the founding members, George Lee of England, Tom Mutters of Germany, and the late G. H. van Dijk of the Netherlands. And during the two decades of the League's existence, an impressive array of distinguished persons from a wide cross-section of professions have helped give us the fighting strength we can muster today. There are the physicians like Drs. Philipson of Sweden, Portray of Belgium, Clemente of Brazil, Beasley of New Zealand, Ben Jafaar of Tunisia, Thorburn of Jamaica; there are the prominent educators and psychologists like John McKenna of Ireland, Henry Cobb of the United States, Peter Mittler of England, Lena Saleh of Jordan, Roger Linster of Luxembourg, and Tor Brandt of Norway. There follow the social scientists and rehabilitation experts led by a real giant in our movement, the late Richard Sterner of Sweden, Allan Roeher of Canada, whose untimely death was such a tragedy, Wehrmeyer of the Netherlands, and Masovic of Yugoslavia. There were the lawyers, Meiresonne of the Netherlands, Maitre Morin of France, and Jose Eguia of Spain, who can lay claim to competence in diverse other fields. There have been the businessmen like Jacques Gemaehling of France, Walter Eigner of Austria, Mr. Raventos of Spain, and Isaac Schemer of Israel. And then, of course, there was the incomparable Yvonne Posternak, the microbiologist, who in her work for her local and national associations as well as for the League gained such competence in our field that the University of Geneva entrusted her with initiating its first special-education program! And if ever I am in a fight, I want her on my side!

So much for a glance at the professions and their representation among the League's leadership. Now I come to another distinguished group of fighters in our cause: Lisa Gyldenkrone of Denmark, Ann Belpaire of Belgium, Eleanor Elkin of the United States, Ingeborg Thomae of Germany, Alda Estrazulas of Brazil, Ewa Garlicka of Poland, Hedy Marmorek of Argentina, all of them not just good and persistent fighters but expert in organizations, pioneers in the field of human services. And somewhere there should be listed a 25-year veteran on the international scene, a woman who has allowed me to become known as Rosemary's husband, and who will be angry with me for all the names I have left out. Those I have mentioned all have been active in the affairs of the League and its member societies, and while most of them are parents of a child with mental handicap, it has by no means been the case with all of them.

I apologize for this lengthy listing, but I hope that for many of you the mention of these names recalled times of trouble, times of progress and of victory in the long struggle on behalf of persons with mental handicap. To be successful in the fight for a cause, there is need for leadership, and, in that respect, our movement indeed has been fortunate.

Just 12 years ago, in neighboring Portugal, the League held a symposium on the development and operation of national societies for the mentally retarded. In her presentation to the symposium, Rosemary Dybwad offered a perspective on historical development. She characterized the 1940s as the time of beginnings of parent groups, most of them fairly closely tied to a particular service, while the 1950s saw the development of strong national organizations. There followed a third phase in the 1960s which she called the decade of sophistication. It brought a more realistic recognition of the immensity of the problem of mental retardation, both in terms of the numbers affected and the multiplicity of services required. The 1960s also saw the formation of the International League of Societies for the Mentally Handicapped. The extremely active and vibrant decade of the 60s also brought the emergence of mentally retarded persons as adults and the recognition of their rights as individuals by the League's Jerusalem Congress. This led to the adoption of the Declaration on the Rights of Mentally Retarded Persons by the United Nations General Assembly. Rosemary correctly predicted for the 1970s that it would be the decade of translating the Declaration into action. "In this process, normalizing the environment and day-to-day life of the mentally retarded individual and safeguarding his personal dignity and integrity will be key factors."

May I now add my own perspective of the 1980s. I think it will be a difficult and problematic time for all our associations, on every level, because we are confronted by our success and must now proceed to translate into broad programs what has been proven by selected demonstration programs. Integration is such an issue, and the turning away from institutions in favor of living in the community. Voting, marriage, and independent living were mere concepts at the Jerusalem Congress but now face us as reality demands, presented by the adults with mental retardation who claim the rights which we proclaimed on their behalf in Jerusalem. Are we ready as societies and as individuals to meet their demands?

On the international scene, the League in similar fashion has had to face up in the 1980s to the realities of the Third World, and I am happy to say we have made great strides. Who among the sophisticated leaders assembled at the League's 1972 Symposium would have dared predict that 10 years later we would assemble for our World Congress in Nairobi, Kenya, deep in the African continent? And as long as our theme is that we need to fight, let me acknowledge as a tough, daring, persistent fighter, Don Mena, who won a battle against a seemingly unending chain of odds, who conquered fiscal uncertainties and official stumbling blocks, to produce an impressive and significant congress. Maybe the League should think of awarding a medal for bravery! But now that we have demonstrated that we can organize effective meetings in Third World countries (and I should add here reference to what we have accomplished in Brassaville and Hong Kong), we face the issue of how we as a League and how our member societies can respond to the needs of what we have come to call the Third World.

Among the recommendations of the 1972 Lisbon Symposium was one related to stages of development that all of our societies tend to go through. It mentioned the third stage of shifting services from the association to statutory authorities, a theme which Wolfensberger so brilliantly elaborated 6 months later at the League's Congress in Montreal. Significantly, you will hear from two of our presenters, Mr. Eigner of Austria and Dr. Thorburn of the Caribbean, some cogent arguments why, in their particular countries, that third stage concept is not a viable solution. When I read their comments I went to my historical file and actually unearthed the report John Fettinger made to the convention of the National Association for Retarded Citizens (USA) in 1958 when he developed the slogan "Our task is to obtain, not to provide." With this historical reference, I want to underline that while we have some issues on which all are ready to fight together in unison, there are other issues on which, for reasons you will hear discussed during this meeting, we have as yet difficulties in arriving at a consensus among ourselves.

You will hear from John Moller of Denmark some reservations about the usual pattern of public school integration, differing from the views of other associations here represented. There may be ample reason for variations in practices from country to country, but it is also quite likely that new evidence gathered in some countries is not being considered in others. Integration, and in particular school integration, is a developmental process, and what last year still seemed quite utopian and impractical may seem much more feasible in the coming year.

I have often spoken of my amazement and my admiration for the early pioneers in our movement who, with a minimum of support, established an effective network of information, so that new insights, new knowledge, new methods could become known quickly across international boundaries and help to bring about desired changes. As our movement has grown, some of our associations maintain major enterprises with large investments, and this can decrease sensitivity to and desire for further change. In any case, one of the real challenges faced by service-giving societies is to set up a system of monitoring its own services and, at the same time, monitoring services provided by governmental agencies. Obviously, this is a difficult task which can easily involve a conflict of interest. I suggest that thought be given to a symposium dealing with this specific problem area.

At the beginning of my remarks, I pointed to the tremendous impression a multinational group of self-advocates had made at the Nairobi Congress and added they were worth fighting for. However, increasingly some of the fighting will be taken care of by them, and indeed, at times, they may be in a better position to fight. I witnessed this in a legislative hearing in my own state of Massachusetts at which several representatives of voluntary associations spoke. It was quite obvious that the senators listened with particular attention and interest to the testimony of a self-advocate. He spoke with great difficulty, but his simple and direct pleading made a deep impression. It has been said before, but it bears repeating, that at the beginning of our movement there was a slogan: "We speak for them." Slowly we have witnessed, as a result of the revolution our movement set into motion, that those for whom we used to speak are beginning to speak for themselves. In Nairobi several of the self-advocates showed themselves capable of speaking for the more severely disabled persons who have not yet gained a voice. But the story I reported from the Massachusetts legislature suggests that indeed some of the persons with handicap may speak effectively for our associations in our fight for change.

Yet I dare ask: How many of our member societies have really seriously considered the recommendations the self-advocacy group put forth in Nairobi? How many have considered ways of making self-advocacy a political reality?

Perhaps we need to consider here a psychological problem. Already at the Lisbon Symposium in 1972 the question was raised "…Who shall determine what constitutes happiness and well-being of the retarded—the parents, professional experts, or the mentally retarded themselves?" Very clearly, one can see in this question the possible seeds of family discord. While parents may philosophically be ready to recognize the adult person with mental handicap, they find it hard to accept this for their own child. By the same token, our member societies may find it hard to accept self-advocates as full partners, or, to stay within our theme, as "comrades-at-arms."

In conclusion, one final concern: *Participation* has become a new watchword in our movement with reference to self-advocates. However, what about participation in the League by the member societies? Earlier I read an honor list (incomplete as it may be) of leaders in our movement. Now that the League's network is spreading ever wider, involving more and more countries and vastly more people, there is danger of an increasing distance between the League and its member societies. The remedy lies in participation, and in particular, active participation in the work of the League's numerous committees. Nothing will more effectively prepare us for the good fight which we must wage together.

CHAPTER 25
LEST WE FORGET

Excerpts from a presentation to the Partners in Progress Conference of the Pennsylvania Association for Retarded Children, Philadelphia, December 1969

I would like to address myself briefly to the theme of your conference: Partners in Progress. And I hope you will let me ask you a very blunt question. What progress? And which partners? Some of you have seen the report of the President's Committee on Mental Retardation 1968, which said that many of the nearly 200,000 residents in state institutions for the mentally retarded live in disgraceful conditions which the state's own regulatory agencies would not tolerate in privately operated facilities for anyone; moreover, that the facilities in which these retarded persons live are in many cases in a state of decay. This is an unusually frank statement for a government report, and yet the very president whose committee wrote these words severely cut the funds for mental retardation, and the new incoming president has cut them yet further, and you are facing a desperate crisis as far as the national programs in mental retardation are concerned. Don't be fooled by the sweet words you are still reading. The mental retardation honeymoon is over, and it is over before the marriage was ever consummated.

We are facing a very tragic situation. Many programs which were started under the impetus of the Kennedy panel and the subsequent legislative action in the Congress are slowly being starved to death. And as you know, it is easier to starve a baby. These programs never had a chance to develop. Practically all professions had wantonly neglected the field of mental retardation. Therefore, whether it was medicine or psychology or education, we needed first of all to train people. For this purpose the Kennedy administration set up legislation to build university-affiliated centers. But now both building and program funds have been cut, and we are facing a great scandal because taxpayers' money has gone into buildings that will be only partially used. The Massachusetts Bureau of Mental Retardation has written a long statement, which we shall gladly make available to you in Pennsylvania, expressing to our congressional delegation and to people in our state and in Washington our extreme concern. And there are, of course, other programs which have been severely curtailed which we desperately need in order to encourage states in the undertaking of new and innovative action. But it is not just the money. The whole attitude has changed and has changed radically. Mental retardation was "in" for a little while, but it is barely hanging on now. And in Pennsylvania after 19 years of work on your part, where are you? You have given the answer yourselves in the statement you have distributed today; there is no need for me to elaborate.

But since you talk about partners, I think a few frank words are needed about that new partnership into which you are going to enter come July through that great new solution of the county mental health and mental retardation program. Permit me to make a prediction. Unless you will decide on drastic, determined, and persistent courses of action—an unlikely eventuality since so many of you are eager to keep the peace and not make waves to disturb what is called political realities—you will 2 years from now face the fact that this new program is the greatest hoax ever perpetrated on the mentally retarded children and adults in Pennsylvania and their families.

Why do I say this? I say this because the whole program obviously is written by the mental health people for the mental health people. Why do I say this? The whole program revolves around psychiatrist and patient, and the great majority of the mentally retarded don't need psychiatrists, and they are not sick. Why do I say it? Because I can safely make the offer here today to donate to the World Federation of Mental Health or to the United Nations Children Fund or to any other worthy cause if you can show me anywhere in the country a single so-called mental health and mental retardation program or a single community mental health and mental retardation center where the mentally retarded are enjoying staff services, facilities, and resources for their own needs on an equal footing with those for the mentally ill and emotionally disturbed.

Let us look at the facts. There has been a constant claim that the mentally retarded child's diagnosis and subsequent treatment, whether residential or nonresidential, must be placed in the hands of psychiatrists. Yet the record shows indisputably that the mentally ill child and the severely emotionally disturbed child in this country have been the subject of continuous severe neglect on the part of the psychiatric profession. Already 9 years ago, at the 1960 White House Conference on Children and Youth, I stated, speaking in my capacity as executive director of the National Association for Retarded Children, that only the mentally ill child was more neglected than the mentally retarded child.

Psychiatry Neglects Retardation

The major blueprint for the development of mental health services in this country is the report of the Joint Commission on Mental Illness and Health, undertaken at the expense of millions of dollars and published shortly before Kennedy's program. It completely left out any consideration of the needs of the mentally ill children. Only just now a new joint commission is at work to remedy this omission, and its report is not yet ready. With such neglect of the mentally ill and emotionally disturbed child, why should psychiatry be so eager to seek control over mental retardation facilities and services? Moreover, what are the particular merits that would qualify psychiatry to assume such a controlling position? I have just come back from the annual conference of the American Psychiatric Association where we had a workshop panel on psychiatry and mental retardation attended by some of the top people of that small group of psychiatrists in this country who work in the field of mental retardation. The consensus was that current philosophy and approaches to training in child psychiatry were not involved with and neglected mental retardation. The entire professional experience in child psychiatry and its clinical orientation goes against the kind of problems encountered in mental retardation. I repeat again, this was the consensus at a meeting last Monday afternoon in Miami at the American Psychiatric Association's convention.

But what about adult psychiatry? Surely these charges, these statements, do not pertain to it. The last two available official federal reports on the activities of adult mental hygiene clinics show that barely 1% of all adults seen at these clinics were mentally retarded individuals. The record is clear. How can you expect much to happen from this kind of partnership? Of course mental health associations and mental health departments will be quick to point out that there is a lack of psychiatrists and psychiatric social workers and clinical psychologists to meet the growing needs of the mentally ill. This is true. How puzzling that in spite of this they are so eager—to put it very mildly—to encompass us. Why should they be so eager that there be joint mental health and mental retardation programs when they don't have enough resources of their own? Why are they pushing us constantly and persistently, openly and even more so behind the scenes? I think the answer is obvious. They want access and control of the appropriations and the resources coming into the mental retardation field.

Let me make one observation based on proven experience in the field to show you this doesn't have to be this way. A very recent report showed that in England a very substantial number of psychiatrists clearly indicated in a professional inquiry they were actively involved in the problem of mental retardation. At the same time an inquiry was made in this country. It showed almost with mathematical accuracy the exact opposite picture: The vast majority of psychiatrists in this country stated in this inquiry that they had no connection—no involvement—with mental retardation. These are facts. Let them be facts; there may be reasons for this, but don't expect a partnership on that kind of basis. Of course what concerns many of us is that this joint mental health and mental retardation program so clearly reflects what we call the "medical model," and what needs to be pointed out clearly is that the "medical model" we are encountering in our institutions is a very poor example of medical practice. I shall gladly accept the challenge to substantiate this.

I do not blame you for being sold down the river by the Mental Health Association and the mental health authorities, but I do blame you a little bit for acting as if it were not so, for acting as if you were enjoying the ride. You have received today, and I hope you have reviewed it carefully—and will review and review and study and study—a very long statement by one of your very fine committees. This has given you a little bit of the state of the nation in terms of the problem of mental retardation in Pennsylvania. Now I think it might be good if we stopped talking a little this noon about what you ought to have and try to find out why it is that you are not getting it. What are the obstacles to change? As your statement said, for 19 years you've tried!

Heavy Institutional Investment

One important inhibiting factor is the tremendous monetary investment your state has in the physical plant of its institutional system and the economic utility this has for certain communities and other interest groups. They attempt to block and effectively delay action for change. This is an unpleasant topic. We do not like to suggest that people make money building institutions—all sorts of people and all sorts of money—money which is not made when funds are used to hire the staff desperately needed in your community to assist families so their children will not have to go to institutions. Certainly the momentum of the current service pattern centering on large institutions is an effective inhibiting source for change.

Looking at this problem from a broad national viewpoint, one can characterize the present development of mental retardation services in the United States somewhat like this: Although there has been a widespread advocacy for increased emphasis on nonresidential services in the community (and certainly you have preached this gospel for more years than you wish to remember), the need for residential services is perpetuated and reinforced by planning low fiscal priorities on nonresidential services and a high fiscal priority on the maintenance of huge outdated institutions and on construction of new institutions. The result is a shortage of nonresidential services which, in turn, leads to the urgency for the creation of additional residential services which are storing up an ever larger number of individuals, since those ready to return to the community cannot be released because of the inadequacy of supportive community services. A vicious circle indeed! This is true all through the nation, reflecting the momentum of the current service pattern. System maintenance is what it is called by the sociologists. For them it is a sociological phenomenon, but for us, a deep tragedy.

Other Factors Inhibit Change

Then of course there are other inhibiting factors to change. Different groups have investments in different services. There certainly are professional groups who have very substantial investments in the present institutional system. They must and do perpetuate themselves: They create new positions which again are slots for people of the same identical professional organization. It is an economic circle; it is a circle of self-interest; and I think it is time we speak out quite freely about it. Enough public documents have been released by these organizations to show how they fear intrusion by others on what they consider as their own preserve.

Yet another inhibiting factor is a very human failing—a denial of reality. The need for change can be effectively repressed by denying unpleasant realities which would underline the urgency for change. When Burton Blatt produced the book *Christmas in Purgatory* (Blatt & Kaplan, 1966), he was attacked: One doesn't do such things. One doesn't expose unpleasant things! It isn't nice. Those who point at institutional atrocities will find themselves more surely attacked than those who commit them.

Maybe I should remind you of something else. As long as we as a nation fail to acknowledge the bitter fact that each night in this, the wealthiest country in the world, tens and tens of thousands of children go to bed hungry, that in our country children die of starvation, we will not take proper action to deal effectively with this problem. That is what Senator McGovern of South Dakota has been trying to tell us, and we are not about to listen, as you know. Again, exactly the same thing has happened to him. He has been maligned and with others has been investigated for speaking out. You just don't say nasty things.

Glossing Over Horrors

As long as you in Pennsylvania and we in Massachusetts and our friends in California continue to gloss over the horrors in our state institutions for the mentally retarded, where defenseless little children are physically attacked, sexually abused, punished in inhuman ways which literally violate the Constitution of the United States; as long as we continue to gloss over these things, there won't be change. When the head of the Danish Mental Retardation Service visited one of California's most advertised institutions, he came out and said that in his country, cattle wouldn't be treated like this. When the head of the Swedish Mental Retardation Services a few weeks ago visited an institution in the state of Massachusetts, he came to me and with a choking voice said, "Don't you ever do that to me again." When the governor of Ohio emerged from one of the visits to a state institution after an inspection, he went to the street curb and vomited, because he was sick to his stomach.

When I was recently asked to come to California during a mental retardation crisis, I was very specific in stressing that the present crisis in the institution could not simply be charged to Governor Reagan's economy measures. I am as opposed to Mr. Reagan's juvenile politics as anyone could be. But the truth is that if not just one but several preceding administrations had not chosen to restrict and starve mental retardation in California—had they not chosen to close their eyes to the prevailing scandalous conditions therefore forcing these programs year by year to the brink of disaster—Mr. Reagan's economy measure would not have endangered health, life, safety of the institution residents to such an extent. You see what I am telling you: For 19 years you have tried to be nice; now you must pay the price for that. You won't simply get rid of your mess by blaming somebody now; you've kept quiet too long....

Harsh Words in a Federal Report

Again, let me remind you. President Kennedy's panel spoke out forthrightly and said the quality of care in our country was highly objectionable and slow to change. *Mental Retardation 1967,* the first report of the President's Committee on Mental Retardation, used much harsher words. It said many of these institutions are plainly a disgrace to the nation and to the state that operates them. Again, in 1968, the President's Committee reported that many of the nearly 200,000 residents in state institutions for the mentally retarded still live in disgraceful conditions, conditions which the state's own regulatory agencies would not tolerate in private facilities.

If a presidential committee report can use this kind of language, why should you have had and continue to have this terrible need of being so desperately polite? You see, we are not attacking individuals: What we are talking about is a system. A system which has been in existence for a long time. You are dealing with the problems engendered by an establishment, a bureaucracy, a professional power structure with various other power structures attached to it and this cannot be blamed on individual persons....

"Plan" Is an Important Step

And now today, you have taken two very important steps. You have adopted "A Plan for Cooperative State Action" and passed a resolution—resolution with which you finally take the first steps to assure for Pennsylvania's retarded citizens some rights in their own country. This resolution to retain counsel to determine what legal action you as an association can take against the Department of Public Welfare to either close Pennhurst or justify its continuance is what you should do. In this country, when a person's rights are violated, we go to the courts for justice. We take legal action. In this instance, legal action has been needed for years. Now you have finally moved on this and I congratulate you....

…We must effectively break the vicious circle and wrest control away from those people who think only of institutions because that is where they find their security. This is the challenge that you face. And now that you have finally come to the conclusion that you must frankly acknowledge the need to call the shots as they are—now that you're finally ready to defend those you always tried to defend but never could—now these alternative actions assume great importance, and I hope sincerely that this day, distinguished by the two decisive actions that you have already taken, will be the most memorable day in the history of PARC [Pennsylvania Association for Retarded Children].

Chapter 26
Self-Determination: Influencing Public Policy

Presentation to the National Self-Determination Conference, Arlington, VA, January 1989

In most books and articles on rehabilitation trends in the United States, the onset of the independent living movement is given as the early 1970s (DeJong, 1983), yet history reads quite differently. In 1957 Rep. Carl Elliott of Alabama, chairman of the Special Education Subcommittee of the House Committee on Education and Labor, introduced H.R. 69-81, which provided for federal funds to the states for the development of independent living services. This legislative proposal came about in response to a resolution adopted in October 1956 by the Delegate Assembly of the National Rehabilitation Association (NRA). E. B. Whitten, the executive director of NRA, welcomed this legislative development enthusiastically in an editorial in the May-August 1957 issue of the *Journal of Rehabilitation*, which ended as follows:

> We believe the time will come when this decision, that State-Federal Support should be made available for independent living rehabilitation services, will be regarded as the initiation of another great forward movement in rehabilitation and in the evolution of the Association toward becoming the organization to which all rehabilitation people look for leadership. (p. 4)

Unfortunately, he spoke too soon: Neither this bill nor a similar one, H.R. 3756, introduced in 1961, which also proposed federal funds for independent living provisions, gained a favorable vote in Congress. It hardly needs emphasizing how much further ahead we would be if federal financing for independent living services would have been available 15 years earlier and, at that, in a period with much more generous financing. Why do I bring these old potatoes to your attention? Because very obviously there had not been enough effort or enough manpower to influence the public policy in question.

The field of rehabilitation in those days was firmly in professional hands. It had been only a few years earlier that the National Rehabilitation Association voted to admit other than professionals to membership. Rehabilitation was as conservative as other human services; the recipients of service had the identity of petitioners rather than of valued collaborators in a common enterprise. Need I say more than to remind you of what happened to Ed Roberts in those very days in California when he was downgraded as "not feasible" for successful rehabilitation, by those who should have served him. But despite his severe physical disability, Ed Roberts had gained for himself a different identity, not that of a dependent client but of a citizen. His self-concept was clear; he did not allow the rehabilitation professionals to downgrade him, and with singular self-determination he forged ahead, his severe physical impairment notwithstanding, and eventually created our country's first center for independent living. In due course, he was appointed by

Governor Brown to be the head of the State Rehabilitation Department that had cast him aside as "not feasible."

The question suggests itself: How was it possible that in a progressive state like California repeated requests for services and equipment from a so obviously bright and alert person as Ed Roberts elicited such negative responses from the rehabilitation authorities? Gerben DeJong (1983), in exploring the reasons why persons with handicaps in general encounter so many obstacles, if not outright rejection, sees the cause in the broad general scene. In an article on "Physical Disability and Public Policy," he wrote:

> The ultimate and most pervasive of environmental barriers are the attitudinal ones, particularly the view that disabled people are helpless, pathetic victims, deserving charitable intervention. There is now more than enough experience to indicate that disabled people can, with appropriate environmental support, lead full and independent lives. Without the removal of attitudinal barriers, the disability legislation of the past decade will not realize its full promise.

To achieve such a basic change in attitude will take precisely what our session today is all about: It will take effective, long-range influencing of public policy on all levels of government—legislative, executive, and judicial—and the action has to come from the persons with disability themselves….

Let me clarify this with some facts from my own experience in the public policy field. On a consultative basis, I had been instrumental in 1968 in suggesting to a committee of the Pennsylvania Association for Retarded Children—deeply concerned about the refusal of schools to admit children with mental retardation and, more yet, about the intolerable neglect and cruelty in state institutions—that since they had over several years tried in vain to get remedial action from the legislature and the administration, the time had come to go to court. The committee was strongly in agreement with that recommendation, but when the matter was brought to the full board of the Association, there was much resistance. After all, it was said, how could the Association dare to sue the secretary of welfare or the head of the state Education Department, on whose goodwill they had to count? In other words, the members of the Association's board saw themselves as clients, depending on the bounty of these departments and their bureaucrats. With such a self-imposed identity, with such a negative self-concept, how could they confront the authorities on whose benevolence they believed they and their children depended?

It took 6 months before the committee chairman, in a very ingenious way…convinced the board members that their parental role, their responsibility toward their children, by far outweighed their relationship with government.

Thus, they came to see themselves in a different light; their self-concept changed, and their resulting self-determination got them to initiate a landmark law suit that resulted in establishing by judicial decree a massive advance in educational policy: No child may be excluded from public education for reasons of handicap, no matter how severe.

Three years later Congress passed Public Law 94-142, the Education of All Handicapped Children Act (1975). It was a singular victory, but unfortunately, not a lasting one. News from throughout the country continues to show that the implementation of this law on the local level is still seriously lagging. Almost everywhere there has been and there still is a need for strong local effort to influence public policy in line with the promise of Public Law 94-142. And the same situation prevails, of course, regarding the keystone to the rights of persons with disability, Section 504 of the 1973 Rehabilitation Amendment and all subsequent amendments.

But how is an effective action program to be initiated and maintained? Rita Varela (1983), writing on "Organizing Disabled People for Political Action," points up that the political realities in our various states differ so very much in terms of local conditions and local leadership that any national campaign must depend on dispersed indigenous leadership to maintain its initial impact. Obviously this necessitates continuing efforts in recruitment and training to gain such leadership. While we have made great progress in using computer programs in teaching technological aspects of work routines, how does one go about helping persons develop a more positive self-concept, leading to a stronger self-determination and to empowerment?

And whence comes this concept of empowerment? I never heard this term used during my years of work in the human services in the 1930s, 40s, and 50s. Not surprisingly, one cannot pinpoint one specific source, but it emanated in part from the struggle in the 1960s around the Model Cities programs and the efforts to give inner-city populations a voice in the councils which directed their fates. Unfortunately, that improvement turned out to be an empty promise, as Stephen Rose (1972) documents in his monograph *The Betrayal of the Poor: The Transformation of Community Action.*

One of the many other examples from that period was the initiative of a group who organized themselves as Mothers on Welfare and who, in the state of Massachusetts, confronted the Department of Welfare, exposing its inadequate and confused as well as confusing practices. Among other successful actions they empowered themselves to write a manual on procedures which the Department had to admit was long overdue. Mothers on Welfare made themselves heard and, notwithstanding their aggressive, confrontational stance, were for the time being accepted as partners by the Department. However, the group, organizationally isolated, lacked the resources to maintain the power it had gained, and slowly faded away.

So what is empowerment?

As one writer states, empowerment takes on a different form in different people and contexts (Rappaport, 1984). Others argue that empowerment is in most instances not a single act but a process. It may start on a rather modest basis but as Douglas Biklen (1988) pointed out in his comments in the TASH Newsletter:

> A wonderful side effect of this empowerment is that it nurtures itself and grows. It produces a system based on self-determination and productivity, i.e., the power of an individual to fully develop his or her potential for a regular life with regular choices. In other words, the empowerment of the advocate results in the empowerment of the consumer—a very simple formula. (p. 1)

I do agree with Biklen but with a very important proviso: Once acquired or activated, the empowerment must be maintained by power sharing, whether through coalition or other support groups, by exchange or accommodation, or else it will dissipate, sooner or later.

Empowerment means that someone or some group or organization acquires or activates power it has not exercised before. But it takes more than having an authority bestowing power; there must be a readiness to take on what may well be not so much a privilege but a burden.

Empowerment may be directed at staff who need this and are organizing to get it from the agency, or it may be directed at the clients, or both groups may work separately or together toward empowerment.

In an article in *Social Policy* entitled "Empowering the Homeless," Michael Fabricant (1988) reports on several smaller voluntary agencies which all have recognized that only by designing a process of empowerment of homeless people who have come for help, can a constructive relationship develop among the client, the social worker, and the agency itself. Homelessness is such an extreme situation that the usual social service agency approach will not work. Most important, the physical surroundings, the demeaning impersonal routines (brought about at least in part by severe overcrowding in the shelters, creating most serious violations of health and housing codes) make clear to the applicants that they are at the bottom of the human scale, powerless and of no use to society. Thus, these agencies on which Michael Fabricant reports set out on a plan of empowerment, on seeking in every way to provide for their clients some choices, and to move away as far as possible from the traditional social service practice of encouraging so-called objectivity by keeping the seekers of aid at a distance. The homeless people in turn come to gain a greater understanding of their own strength and develop a sense of self-determination and empowerment which results in a greater capacity to challenge the conditions of their life.

It is important to note that the agencies involved in this study were not large, bureaucratic entities, but small nongovernmental units where such radical alteration of routines was feasible. A pervasive question remains: Can our ruling bureaucracies, can our legislative bodies, comprehend and support such a radical departure from the traditional pattern of service provision?

A significant new venture in the arena of empowerment has been undertaken by the Governor's Planning Council on Developmental Disabilities in Minnesota under the title Partners in Policymaking. Observing the marked decline in active participation by parents of children with developmental disabilities in public affairs, especially in planning and in legislation, the council has established a rather intensive training program for citizens, including parents of children with developmental disabilities and also some self-advocates. It aims at giving them an understanding of today's issues and of ways to acquire a power base from which to advocate. Participants are reimbursed for their expenses but must obligate themselves to attend all the sessions and training events. The expectation is that after the course many of these parents, having sought empowerment, will play a role in improving services, in pushing for legislation, and in locating and pursuing instances of inadequate attention to the special needs of people with disabilities. The results so far are encouraging and new voices are being heard in Minnesota.

I think you will agree that among deprived, disenfranchised groups in our country, the residents of mental retardation institutions are near the bottom. But even from there comes a new strength, a self-determination, a new voice of self-generated empowerment. Just a few weeks ago, a group of residents of the Southbury Training School in Connecticut asked some of their friends in the community to arrange for a press conference. This was held at the institution. Most of the larger Connecticut newspapers carried an account, some on the front page, about these self-empowered institutional residents appealing to the public for justice and termination of their institutional confinement.

So far my comments have dealt with empowerment directed at social action. But the empowerment of individuals toward leading a richer life, toward greater self-fulfillment, certainly is for many of us at least of equal concern.

One of the oldest stratagems in the disability movements had been the one-to-one approach to parents—

whether it was called Pilot Parents, Parent-to-Parent, or, as in France, L'Action Interfamiliale (Interfamily Action). In Massachusetts I encountered already in 1958 a well-functioning program called Parent Resource Persons. These programs remain effective even where there are relatively full service programs, because they can give parents who have never had or sought outside help the courage to do so.

As the disability movement matured, the focus included more and more the persons with disability themselves, highlighting personal adjustment struggles often by far exceeding those of parents. Into this challenging area has come this very month a beacon of light, a new book by our friends Robert and Martha Perske (1989). Its title tells it all: *Circle of Friends: Persons With Disabilities and Their Friends Enrich the Lives of One Another*. Essentially, it is a series of vignettes showing how human beings are being helped to develop or regain the power they need to cope. It is a gripping, realistic book, but, like all the work of Bob and Martha, there is a beauty and serenity about it.

For our discussion today, the book has a specified meaning because one of its vignettes shows how Judith Snow, whom I have known from my work with the G. Allen Roher Institute in Toronto for a number of years, at one point no longer could cope alone with her existence in a wheelchair, with only one thumb functioning. She had been active in education and the human services, but problems became too much for her and she virtually collapsed. At that point, a circle of friends formed around her—it is a gripping story to read—and now she is back at work and both the Canadian government and the Canadian Association for Community Living value her as a leading expert on the political and social situation of persons with disabilities.

Again we need to recognize that self-determination as much as empowerment cannot continue indefinitely without strong positive reinforcement, a recharging of the batteries, so to speak. This crucial point needs to be heeded in the long-range planning of social action, such as the implementation of significant, broad legislative advances.

Circle of Friends is one figure of speech. Bridge building and building community are others. From Communitas, Inc., a Connecticut group, has just come a contribution entitled *What Are We Learning About Bridge Building? A Summary of a Dialogue Between People Seeking to Build Communities for People With Disabilities* (Mount, Beeman, & Ducharme, 1988). It is more of a how-to book, also focusing on how to enable individuals with handicap to gain the power to cope with life.

Throughout my long friendship with Robert Perske, he has time and again redirected my thinking into new and innovative channels, and he does so with formulations which at first sound so very simple until you begin to fully understand their significance. Let me then quote from his concluding words in *Circle of Friends*:

> As people talk to each other, persons with disabilities have been able to contribute their own unique richness to their friends and to the surrounding neighborhoods as well. Therefore, I believe that friendships with people who have disabilities can provide an explosion of fresh values and directions which this confused, misdirected world needs now as never before. (p. 91)

Chapter 27
The Revolutionary Vision Unfolds

Presentation at the 19th Annual Conference, Continue the Revolution, National Down Syndrome Congress, Boston, September 1991

May I bring you first of all, warmest greetings from the International League of Societies for Persons With Mental Handicap and from its president, Victor Wahlstrom of Stockholm, Sweden. With associations in more than a hundred countries across all continents, the League unites parents on a truly worldwide basis as is also demonstrated by its congresses—the last four having met in Vienna, Austria; Nairobi, Kenya; Rio de Janeiro, Brazil; and Paris, France. I have been very pleased by your editor's efforts to include in *Down Syndrome News* information on Down syndrome developments in other countries, and I hope many of you appreciate that progress in the field of disability must be our concern in today's world, not just on the local, state, and national levels, but also in the international level.

Your program committee has requested that for this congress with the theme Continue the Revolution, I present some introductory remarks titled "The Revolutionary Vision Unfolds." For one who has worked in this field for more than 50 years, that is a broad-gauged but rewarding challenge, because I very much agree with Maureen Babula, who, in her editorial in the last issue of *Down Syndrome News*, said, "When one is feeling really frustrated and depressed about a child's progress, look back—think of what that youngster has already accomplished—things that you once completely despaired of ever seeing" (1991, p. 85).

So let me look back to my first encounter with Down syndrome, in 1938 at the New York State institution at Letchworth Village, a dreary depressing place with more than 3,000 residents, where at that time I found dormitories crowded with 100 beds and 125 children in those hundred beds. Many of those children spent a few hours in school, but not one with Down syndrome, which then still was known as mongolism; it was a well-established fact that "mongoloids," as they were called, were not capable of benefiting from any school program.

Let me be frank: My 3 months at Letchworth Village were a dulling experience, and I was glad to return to the institution for juvenile offenders where I was working at the time, an institution which was far better staffed and provided for better housing, equipment, and nutrition than did Letchworth Village. In the 1940s I became director of child welfare for the state of Michigan, and I began to hear some of the child welfare workers' reports of groups of parents whose children were mentally defective (and again I am using the language of those days) but who were insistent on gaining some programs for them. And soon enough the dam broke and the local groups banded together, formed nationally the National Association for Retarded Children, and then the United Cerebral Palsy Association, and the revolution started. There is no time here today to recount those early days when their accumulated anger at having their children excluded from school and all manner of community life and their determination to bring about radical change enabled these parents to move bureaucratic mountains and defeat professional indolence. The revolution was here and in the course of the 1950s got firmly established. The wisdom, tactical skill, dogged persistence, and personal commitment of those parent pioneers were awe-inspiring, but they were also successful in gaining increasing interest and support from members of relevant professions. And parent leaders like Elizabeth Boggs developed a vision that would carry these early victories toward legislation and the establishment of a network of services.

The new decade of the 1960s brought the Kennedy initiative in the form of the President's Panel on Mental Retardation. By implication, there was a disavowal of the stormy parent action mode and the panel proceeded along fairly conservative lines. In retrospect it is interesting that the panel in no way envisioned a major role for the family, nor was the significance of the parental rebellion of the late 40s reflected in the panel's report.

In the context of Down syndrome, however, the late 50s and early 60s were of great importance in my judgment, because it was in those years that Dr. Richard Koch and his staff at the Los Angeles Children's Hospital began to challenge prevailing universally negative views about the intellectual, emotional, and social competence of children with Down syndrome. I was, in those days, a frequent visitor at their clinic, and they certainly revolutionized my thinking and that of many of my colleagues. Many of you will remember him from the early beginnings of the Down Syndrome Congress. His legacy, his revolutionary vision, has been unfolding under the untiring leadership of another "patron saint" of the Down Syndrome Congress, Dr. Siegfried Pueschel. Theirs has been a quiet revolution, but both men excelled in their ability to communicate with parents, one from the West Coast and the other from the East Coast, and I am happy to tell you that on my international travels I see increasing evidence how Dr. Pueschel's revolutionary vision is unfolding in other lands as well. Through almost 25 years, he has exercised in his quiet, all too modest way, a leadership which must be credited at least in part with the phenomenal progress that has been made on behalf of the young child and adolescent with Down syndrome. And I hope you will allow me to add with local pride that his work got its start at the Development Evaluation Clinic so ably directed here in Boston at the Children's Hospital.

While the work of Dr. Koch and his associates and that of similar clinics established in the 1960s with funds from the United States Children's Bureau effectively reinforced the revolutionary visions of the parent revolt, the response from the educational field was disappointingly negative. I remember a conference of the Council for Exceptional Children when Dr. James Baldini, a research chemist from Delaware and chairman of National Association for Retarded Children's Education Committee, issued this challenge to the educators present: "Why do you always assume that our children cannot learn, could it not be that you do not yet know how to teach them?" As you can imagine, his comment was not well accepted, but as a research worker he made a valid contention; today, of course, schools successfully educate children deemed ineducable in those days. I have in my files a relevant clipping from the *Journal of Rehabilitation* of November 1960, titled "Dr. Koch Comments: Public Ahead of Professionals." It quotes Dr. Koch, then professor of special education at the University of Illinois and author of a leading textbook, as follows:

> The public has gone so fast in their demands on what should be done with the mentally retarded in all areas—medical, social, educational, and otherwise—that today we find not so much a

cultural lag, but really a professional lag. Those of us in the professional field find ourselves so overwhelmed with not only demands but sometimes support that we don't have the people today to handle this in a high professional level; and I think that can be said for all the professional groups rather than just one of them.

In other words, the parents' revolutionary vision of their children's admission to the public schools was seen as too far advanced to meet with much response. But then help came from an unexpected political source: President Johnson's interest in civil rights and in the war against poverty resulted in the passage in 1965 of the Elementary and Secondary Education Act, which for the first time ever made federal funds available to local school systems including educational services for disadvantaged youth.

But response in the states remained slow, and 1969 witnessed another pioneering parent initiative: The Pennsylvania Association for Retarded Children in federal court sued the Pennsylvania educational authorities to provide special education for all children with mental retardation. They won in 1972 a significant consent decree which firmly established that all children, bar none, had a right to education.

Three years later in 1975 Congress passed Public Law 94-142, the Education for All Handicapped Children Act, which has since been extended in its coverage by several amendments with particular attention to the early educational needs of children with disabilities.

Also—although the revolutionary vision of those early parent pioneers has thus become more and more clarified and reinforced as a definitive national policy, spelled out in the federal statutes, implementation on the local level (i.e., response from the local school authorities) has been badly lagging.

To be sure, throughout the country, one can today find school systems which have established programs that appropriately meet the needs of children with handicap, and *Down Syndrome News* regularly carries news items regarding such developments. But while they prove that the requirement of the law can be met, these positive examples unfortunately represent but a tiny fraction of school districts nationwide.

The time is long overdue for a concerted nationwide drive to close this intolerable gap between a clearly expressed national political resolve and the failure of local authorities to comply. Each of us in this room this morning needs to stop and think: "What am I doing in *my* local community to have this national educational mandate realized?" And let no one tell you that in our present fiscal predicament we must exercise patience when it comes to extending schooling for children with severe disabilities. To such a view, Judge Waddy of the United States District Court in Washington, DC, gave a clear answer almost 25 years ago on August 1, 1972, in the case of *Mills v. Board of Education* in these words:

> If sufficient funds are not available to finance all of the services and programs that are needed and desirable in the system then the available funds must be expended equitably in such a manner that no child is entirely excluded from a publicly supported education consistent with his needs and ability to benefit therefrom. The inadequacies of the District of Columbia Public School system, whether occasioned by insufficient funding or administrative inefficiency, certainly cannot be permitted to bear more heavily on the "exceptional" or handicapped child than on the normal child.

Four decades have passed in the struggle to gain full educational rights for all—obviously we need to give thought to more effective strategies.

So far, I have dealt with visions from past revolutions, but in our vibrant, ever-changing field we must be prepared to deal with emerging revolutions which may bring us new visions of changes greatly affecting our work and the lives of those we aim to assist. One such emerging revolution was sketched out by Clarence Sundram, chairman of the New York State Commission on the Quality of Care, in an article he entitled "Regulation—Have We All Gone Mad?" (1988). Over the past years, everyone actively involved in this field, whether as parent, recipient of services, counselor, case manager, or provider, is faced with a mountain of paperwork prescribed as the result of mountains of regulations, all supposedly geared to enhance health and safety, to protect rights, and to improve the quality of life. And they all require ample documentation in quadruplicate. There are, for example, regulations which supposedly protect the privacy of persons, but in effect it is the rules which invade the person's privacy and interfere with his quite acceptable lifestyle. Among the questions Clarence Sundram raises are these: Who is it we are trying to protect, and what is it we are trying to protect against? Are all the interests we are trying to protect important, and do they really need protection? And, significantly, what are the costs—both direct and indirect—of trying to protect these interests? There are regulations (many related to financing care) which actually turn out to be disincentives to undertake natural and cost effective home care, or which make working financially disadvantageous. Or they require (as is the case in Massachusetts) a nurse to be engaged for a contractually established minimum of hours for the sole purpose of giving a person living in a community residence a medication which can be purchased over the counter. Obviously there were initially good reasons for the primary regulations, but for too many employees they form the essence of their work and, thus, are not just to be protected but to be built up and enhanced by more detail, at the risk of neglecting the very individual they were initially to protect. Obviously time does not permit this morning to dwell on ways to meet these problems, but I did want to point out that we need to recognize that things around us may well come to a point where drastic change must be undertaken.

Inevitably the unfolding of the original revolutionary visions of the pioneers in our movement will take us into aspects and territories not foreseen by them. I well remember from the early 1950s a widely distributed leaflet titled "We Speak for Them." It was more than a slogan. It was a battle cry, an assertion of parental competence and commitment against a domineering state bureaucracy and the equally domineering voice of certain professional groups….

CHAPTER 28
TRANSITIONS IN ACTION: IMPACT ON THE PLANNING PROCESS

Excerpt from presentation by Rosemary and Gunnar Dybwad at The Third Interamerican Congress on Mental Retardation, Buenos Aires, Argentina, August 1986

Our task for this morning is to talk with you on the topic "Transitions in Action: Impact on the Planning Process." This is a challenging assignment, because all of us involved in this field have witnessed and continue to witness remarkable transitions—transitions in the lives of persons with mental handicap and their families, and in the way society views them and provides for them. We decided to divide the topic in this manner: Rosemary would explore the roles played in the planning process by the individual parents, by the persons with mental handicap, and by associations of parents and friends. Then I would follow with a discussion of impacts on the planning process of the service systems such as schools, institutions, community health and welfare agencies, the societal impact of the family as a social system.

From previous experience we anticipate that some of our statements may be, to some of you, disturbing, or indeed offensive, reflecting our fantasy and wishful thinking. We admit we have been dreaming and scheming for a good many years. Yet looking back over the past three decades, we find that we have been too timid in our dreaming, and that reality has time and again overtaken our dreams and pushed developments in this field much further ahead than we thought possible. This is the case—relatively speaking—all over the world. As my wife and I read newsletters of associations, public documents, and informal reports of traveling friends, we are time and again amazed about the advances taking place.

We continue of course to face lack of funds, lack of resources, lack of personnel, as well as lack of knowledge and skills. Ann Shearer, well-known British journalist and cofounder of the Campaign for Mentally Handicapped People, has an important message on that score. She is the author of a publication written for the International League of Societies for Persons With Mental Handicap, entitled *Think Positive: Advice on Presenting People With Mental Handicap*. With numerous examples she shows how unfavorable news can safely be presented as long as it is within a positive context. All too often negative aspects about the situation in the field of mental retardation are reported in a way that reflects unfavorably on the persons with mental handicap whether they are in residential institutions, in community homes, or in schools, etc. Individuals are discussed as problems rather than persons.

In a world where many people still don't accept fellow-citizens who have a mental handicap as equally-respected members of their communities, [parent associations] could play a special part in combating old fears and prejudices and in presenting a new view of "what people with mental handicap are like." ...There is no such thing as a neutral image of a person who has a mental handicap. Unless it is deliberately made positive, people will see it as confirming their negative preconceptions—whether that is intended or not. And because negative images are so powerful and deep, it takes very deliberate thought and action to combat them. (1984b, pp. 3-4)

I strongly recommend to all working in our field, parents and professionals alike, this pamphlet of Ann Shearer's, available from the International League: *Think Positive*.

Parents

If we look at parents of persons with mental handicap as policy makers and at their role in the planning process, we can see three well-defined areas. The first is the immediate responsibility of the parent to plan for their handicapped child day by day, year by year. The second is the role of the parent in the organizational structure of their own parent association on the local, provincial, or national level. Thirdly, as we move from form and structure to the substance of the parent association, we see a collective parental impact on the total service system, legal provision, and fiscal ramifications.

In the early days, the 1940s and 50s, there was little room for the parents of a child with substantial handicap to consider planning options, to make choices, or even to have hopes. Those were the days when children with mental handicap who did live at home were practically kept hidden, because such parents found themselves cut off from the normal societal opportunities. As a matter of fact, it was this lack of opportunities, this inability to make choices other parents could make, that brought about the revolt of the parents and the spontaneous formation, within a time frame of very few years, of the parent movement in countries throughout the world.

There were two other factors in those early days that affected the parental role in the planning process. The first was the presumption of a much shortened life span for persons with mental handicap, with the consequent presumption that the parent was likely to outlive his offspring, and the second, an even more significant presumption that the child would never grow, would never develop. As a consequence, parents saw it as their duty, as their moral as well as practical responsibility, to assume complete personal control of their child even when he became an adult in years. In societies where such facilities existed, this included the choice of permanently entrusting the child to the care of a residential institution.

Today the situation has radically changed. Parents have found that even the most severely handicapped child can and does grow and learn, and that they will need help and assistance to meet his needs and potential.

As the education system increasingly is ready to serve such children (and indeed we now have countries where the education authorities must serve every child, no matter how severely handicapped) these children are brought into societal living, begin to face and interact with the community. Schooling is followed by vocational training, and slowly, all too slowly, by employment opportunities other than in the controlled environment of the sheltered workshop.

Increasingly in some of the more advanced countries, adults with mental handicap earn wages, live away from their parental home, not just in the more or less controlled group home, but in an apartment shared perhaps with one or two others. Indeed he may want to share his abode with a person of the opposite sex and get married, with or without his parents' blessing. All of this has brought the most profound change in the interpersonal relationships in families with a mentally handicapped son or daughter and, of course, imposes on parents a very difficult and sometimes almost impossible responsibility: to allow the child to move into adult status and yet continue to provide guidance, support, and perhaps even a certain amount of control.

While we have had schemes like Parent Resource Persons, Parent-to-Parent programs and Interfamily Action for many years, they have dealt primarily with day-to-day problems in the care of the child with handicap. The vastly expanded opportunities (but also risks) that are opening up for the adult person with mental handicap bring about a need for a more sophisticated type of parental planning, and the need for help from other more knowledgeable persons.

Right at this time in several countries a variety of schemes are being worked out to make it possible for parents to participate actively in planning and providing housing for their adult son or daughter, rather than to leave this job to the state bureaucracy. While the development of trusts has been primarily furthered by more well-to-do families, increasingly such schemes will be desired by more and more families. Cooperative planning by a small group of families is another possibility much under discussion.

International Variation

In all of this we see of course a tremendous variation from country to country. Increasing industrialization in Third World countries brings with it migration and a diminishing role of the extended family in caring for persons with handicap. On the other hand, in other countries we find in most recent years a greater readiness of brothers and sisters to assume a share of the family responsibility and often this deals more with planning than with day-to-day guidance and supervision.

In general, when there is talk about the planning process one does not think of the average family, yet the foregoing comments have pointed out that rearing a child with a severe handicap has become, under the impact of the new developments, a challenge in planning.

In an international meeting the question may well be raised: What meaning has all this talk about planning services for children and adults with mental handicap in a country where the average child in rural areas has at best just a few years of schooling, where there is lack of even the most basic health care, and where only the rich have access to services? Yet even parents who live under the most deprived circumstances have dreams and hopes for their children, and once these parents join with others, dreams and hopes can form a political agenda for the future. Furthermore, as we were able to observe, for instance in various places in India, the private school organized by well-to-do parents for the benefit of their own children becomes a demonstration to the authorities and the community of what can be done and a place of training for an initial cadre of staff to develop services on a broader basis.

A theme that can be observed in much of the literature contributed so richly by parents of children with mental handicap in various countries has been the movement from initial parental grief to an all-out effort to assist the child's development and to a final reaching out to join others in mutual aid and eventually political action. The major tool for this has been the establishment of parent associations. Their origin has had significant similarity from country to country, invariably involving a parent whose frustration had exceeded the bearable. There are of course significant differences from association to association even within countries, involving the planning process. There are, for example, those associations which build the original self-help project of the founding parent group into a major network of services. Others see danger in being in the continuing role of a provider (which means usually being the recipient of government funds) and instead see their role as advocates for the individual child or in more general political action. More recently some associations are in the process of planning a system of monitoring services for quality, consistency, and accessibility.

Furthermore, the rapid growth of organizational movements in all disabilities presents another planning challenge: To what extent does one yield identity and goals of one's own organization to gain strength and political influence by joining a coalition or a specific cooperative enterprise with other disability organizations? And how does one plan to attract new members from among young parents who, with their disabled child, have benefited from the newly developed services and have not experienced the despair and frustration which led to the founding of the association? These and related problems were discussed in 1984 at a symposium of the International League of Societies for Persons With Mental Handicap dealing with the future role of voluntary associations. A report on this conference is available from the League.

The public record shows that through the voice of the associations they have created, parents of the mentally handicapped children have had a significant impact on governmental policy and formal and informal community development. The underlying planning process is becoming more difficult as we move from the correction of obviously unjust and abusive situations to a higher level, including, for instance, early intervention services brought to the family's residence, as compared with an emphasis on work training and supported work placements in open employment. In other words, in selecting planning priorities, the associations today face difficult choices about competing interests within their organization—a price of the progress that has brought us more and varied opportunities.

One of the most moving experiences for someone who has worked in the field of mental handicap for many decades is to see and hear an individual with mental handicap appear before a parliamentary committee or a city council, either to favor or to protest a particular measure, speaking awkwardly, searching for words, yet able to give some answer to questions put by members of the legislative body. Here is another scenario that would have met with total disbelief, indeed ridicule, in the early years of the parent movement, but today in an increasing number of countries with quite different cultural traditions, an essential part of the planning process in our field has become the inclusion of persons with mental handicap at some point in the deliberations.

Rights of Mentally Retarded People

This new extension of the planning process is of such significance that it might be well for us to take a second look as to how this came about. It was not until the 1960s that the first articles appeared, recognizing that mentally retarded children grow up to be adults. At the League's Third Congress held in 1966 in Paris the final summarization included this statement: "And clearly into focus came at the Congress the retarded adult, a member of society, endowed with both natural and political rights, which no one may curtail but for good and valid cause, in proceedings which protect his interest, no matter how profoundly handicapped he may be."

It was in this spirit that the League decided that the theme of its next Congress, to be held in Jerusalem in 1968, should be From Charity to Rights, and that in preparation a symposium should be held in Stockholm in 1964 on the topic Legislative Aspects of Mental

Retardation. The published Conclusions of the Stockholm Symposium (International League, 1967) included a section on individual rights, with the following introductory statement:

III. INDIVIDUAL RIGHTS

The Symposium considered that no examination of the legislative aspects of the problem of mental retardation would be complete without general consideration being given to the basic rights of the mentally retarded, not only from the standpoint of their collective rights and those of their families, but also from that of the individual rights of the retarded person as a human being. The Symposium affirmed the following:

III.1 General principles

a. The mentally retarded person has the same rights as other citizens of the same country, same age, family status, working status, etc., unless a specific individual determination has been made, by appropriate procedures, that his exercise of some or all of such rights will place his own interest or those of others in undue jeopardy. Among the rights to which this general principle may apply are: the right to choose a place to live, to engage in leisure time activities, to dispose of property, to preserve the physical and psychological integrity of his person, to vote, to marry, to have children, and to be given a fair trial for any alleged offense.

b. The retarded person has, furthermore, a right to receive such special training, rehabilitation, guidance and counseling as may strengthen his ability to exercise these rights with the minimum of abridgment.

There followed other provisions which I need not quote in this context, but I do wish to call your attention to this historical document, available from the League.

It was in the spirit of the Stockholm conclusions that Henry V. Cobb, the League's president, said in his welcoming address at the Jerusalem Congress a year later:

> We are met here to reaffirm the fundamental right of the mentally retarded to a life of decency and dignity. In this affirmation we are not speaking as citizens of any country, though we come from many countries; we are not speaking as adherents to any faith or creed, though we hold many faiths and creeds; we are not speaking in the terms of our own language, though we speak in many tongues. We are making an affirmation that transcends all nationalities, all races, all creeds, and faiths, and tongues....
>
> To all here assembled, may I welcome you to share with us in our united determination to lift the mentally retarded from the shadows into the sunlight—not as an act of charity but as an affirmation of human right.

Thus stimulated, the Congress proceeded to fashion the Conclusions of the Stockholm Symposium into a Declaration of General and Special Rights of the Mentally Retarded. It is noteworthy that the drafters of this Declaration did not go along quite all the way with the Symposium's recommendations. Left out from the Declaration were the references to the right to choose a place to live, to dispose of property, to vote, to marry, and to have children. It was felt that these statements went too far beyond what the public could accept at that point.

So far things had moved in line with the League's planning process, but not even the most audacious, most optimistic of its leaders would have dared to predict what followed. In 1971 the United Nations General Assembly adopted, without a dissenting vote, this Declaration with some textual changes, the most significant being the addition of the word *persons* in the Declaration's title (Declaration on the Rights of Mentally Retarded Persons, December 20, 1971).

This surprising action by the United Nations was hailed as a great victory at the League's Montreal Congress the following year, but in her opening address the League's president, Yvonne Posternak, also pointed out that this great Declaration had no binding force on any government and that therefore the League would have to make every effort to have the Declaration accepted at least in spirit by the various governments. Accordingly the League formed a Task Group on the Implementation of Rights. Eventually this Task Group published in four languages a booklet entitled *Step by Step: Guidelines on Implementation of the Declaration on the Rights of Mentally Retarded Persons* (International League, 1978).

Meanwhile, first in Sweden and then in several other countries, groups of persons with mental retardation had actually begun meeting, demonstrating that they were quite capable of expressing their hopes and wishes for their own way of living, and of commenting on services provided for them. That stimulated discussions on how this could be included in training programs. Thus the League selected as theme for its next Congress the simple word *Choices*. Thus the Vienna Congress (1978) explored both how to provide opportunities to make decisions, to make choices, for persons with mental retardation, beginning in infancy, and how they could learn to make decisions regarding life choices. The Congress also emphasized the importance of new choices and decisions to be made by parents and professionals as well as society itself if persons with handicaps are to be truly accepted as fellow human beings and fellow citizens.

This whole planning process of the League came to fruition at its International Congress in 1982 in Nairobi, when eight people with mental handicap managed a full morning's plenary session, including an unrehearsed question and answer period with a large audience from 70 different countries.

There is no more significant transition in action in the field of mental handicap, and its impact on the planning process will steadily grow in significance.

Chapter 29
Using the Courts

Excerpt from a presentation, "The Undeveloped Resource at the Edge of Change," at the Fall Conference on Mental Retardation, cosponsored by the California Council for Retarded Children and the American Association on Mental Deficiency, San Francisco, November 1968

I would like to make a suggestion to you. The governor of a state is not a person who can act on his own; he is facing, and has to work with, distinguished citizens of the state who represent the highway lobby, distinguished citizens of the state who represent the retail merchants lobby, and so on and so on. I need not take your time by reciting this. So maybe some time you need to get a little help for the governor by more vigorously recruiting a lobby from the general public on behalf of the retarded. And I would say if we cannot get administrative relief, if the administration assures us that they do not see how they can do more, that they do all they can do, let us use an important traditional weapon our system of government makes available to us. Let us go to the courts.

Some very interesting things are happening in this country. A little while ago, the Supreme Court, on the petition of an individual, issued a very important decision—the *Gault* decision—which is resulting in a very radical change in the way in which we are treating juvenile delinquents in this country. Administrative relief had not been forthcoming. Somebody went to the court. The court reaffirmed certain principles, and now we have change.

In Washington, DC, there recently has been a case known as *Rouse v. Cameron*—Dr. Cameron being a world-famous psychiatrist who is the superintendent of Saint Elizabeth's Hospital. A particular person being confined there—confined as a mentally ill person against his will—went to court and claimed that he was confined illegally because he had been confined there for treatment but was not getting any treatment. The court upheld this view and, significantly, was supported by the American Orthopsychiatric Association—one of our most distinguished multidisciplinary professional organizations of which our leading child psychiatrists and adult psychiatrists, psychologists, social workers, and therapists, are members. The Association filed a brief as friend of the court pointing out that they agreed with the main point that was on debate: Is it feasible for a court to arrogate upon itself the right to decide what is treatment or not? In a very reasonable and well-reasoned, rather conservative way, they said very definitely the courts can establish a certain frame of reference as constituting the minimum essentials of treatment and anything outside of it just is not treatment. Of course once such a court decision is issued, the administration has a mandate far stronger than any mandate even the combined voluntary organizations could ever lay on the desk of the governor.

It just so happens that exactly 3 days ago in Boston a similar suit was filed, this time on behalf of a juvenile delinquent and different from the Supreme Court's *Gault* decision that dealt with juvenile court procedures. This case deals with methods of treatment in a state institution, and the court petitions set forth very clearly that what was happening in that institution constituted inadequate treatment without any doubt and that, therefore, this young man would have the right to his freedom. Since, obviously, he should not have his freedom because he needs some constraining influence, it is very clear that the state will have to act on this and bring about change.

I am sorry that there is no time to discuss here the Bill of Rights of the Mentally Retarded which was passed in the presence of some eminent people from California at the recent International Congress of the International League of Societies for the Mentally Handicapped. This whole concept that the mentally retarded have basic human rights, and, furthermore, that these human rights could be enforced is a very new one, but it is coming. At various times I have urged administrators of state programs to read carefully the "signs on the wall" before they become subject to emanating judicial interference....

Chapter 30
"A Debt of Gratitude"

*From "Introduction," 1983, Western New England Law Review, 5 (3), 323-336,
reprinted with permission*

It has been nearly 15 years since I met with a group from the Pennsylvania Association for Retarded Children at Brandeis University's Florence Heller Graduate School to develop a plan of action intended to alleviate the abuse and neglect rampant in Pennsylvania's state mental retardation institutions and to curb exclusionary practices which denied many thousands of Pennsylvania's children the right to a minimal level of elementary education. Until that time, the Association's efforts to improve the level of state services had included meetings with the secretary of welfare, appearances before legislative committees supported by experts of international reputation, and efforts to increase citizen awareness and governmental action through the media. All these efforts to improve the quality of services to persons with disabilities and handicaps had failed. The realization of this failure led those present to an unexpected conclusion: Because the executive and legislative branches of the state government had not succeeded to bring relief to the myriads of wronged Pennsylvanian children and their families, it was time to take the problem to the courts and to invoke the corrective powers of the judiciary.

The ensuing action in federal court, *Pennsylvania Association for Retarded Children v. Pennsylvania*,[1] became a landmark case in the struggle to secure a right to education for children with mental retardation. This case was closely followed by *Mills v. Board of Education of the District of Columbia*[2] which extended this right to include children with all types of disabilities. Both of these cases created the foundation for a series of similar litigation around the country, calling for decisive changes in the education of children with handicaps.[3]

Contemporaneously, *Wyatt v. Stickney*[4] broke new ground for another series of cases concerned with the right to treatment, and the right to protection from harm and the imposition of peonage in the massive mental retardation institutions which confined children

---

[1] 343 F. Supp. 279 (E.D. Pa. 1972), *modifying*, 334 F. Supp. 1257 (E.D. Pa. 1971).

[2] 348 F. Supp. 866 (D.D.C. 1972).

[3] For cases involving the right to education for children with retardation, *see, e.g.*, Armstrong v. Kline, 476 F. Supp. 583 (E.D. Pa. 1979), *remanded sub nom.*, Battle v. Pennsylvania, 629 F.2d 269 (3d Cir. 1980), *cert denied sub nom.*, Scanlon v. Battle, 452 U.S. 968 (1981); Fialkowski v. Shapp, 405 F.2d 946 (E.D. Pa. 1975); Harrison v. Michigan, 350 F. Supp. 846 (E.D. Mich. 1972). For cases broadening the right to education to include children with all types of disabilities, *see, e.g.*, Board of Educ. v. Rowley, 102 S. Ct. 3034 (1982); Tonya K. v. Chicago Bd. of Educ., 551 F. Supp. 1107 (N.D. Ill. 1982); Davis v. District of Columbia Bd. of Educ., 522 F. Supp. 1102 (D.D.C. 1981); Panitch v. Wisconsin, 371 F. Supp. 955 (E.D. Wis. 1974).

[4] 334 F. Supp. 1341 (M.D. Ala. 1971), *orders entered*, 344 F. Supp. 373 (M.D. Ala. 1972) (order for mental illness facilities), *aff'd in part, rev'd and remanded in part sub nom.*, Wyatt v. Aderholt, 503 F.2d 1305 (5th Cir. 1974).

and adults under conditions inferior to and more repressive than those in our prison systems.[1]

These lawsuits have been the subject of considerable controversy and the ensuing court orders have been characterized as unnecessary intrusions by the judiciary, largely ineffectual, and unsound in the day-to-day practice. I strongly dissent from such negative appraisal of these developments over the past 10 years. The legal process exposed, as nothing else could have, the truly incredible record of human abuse and neglect and of governmental irresponsibility and indifference.

One example must suffice: Blatt and Kaplan (1966) had provided the nation with a pictorial presentation of institutional abuse that subsequently was featured in *Look* (Blatt & Mangel, 1967), one of the most popular magazines of the time. Sen. Robert Kennedy followed this presentation with a strong televised message about the inhuman conditions existing at the Willowbrook institution in New York. But neither the public nor the involved professional associations in the field of psychiatry, psychology, or social welfare felt called upon to insist on remedial action. The problem was, as one observer noted, "eyes that see not, ears that hear not, minds that deny the evidence before them" (Sarason, 1969, p. 345). It remained for the courts to force decisive action.

Yet the questions persist. Is the tremendous expense of public moneys, this gross disruption of ongoing administration and service delivery, and the encroachment of executive decisions and professional judgments really justified by the results obtained? The most compelling answer to this query comes from the countless number of those who, as a result of the court's actions, are finally receiving the education so long denied them and from those who are freed from institutional abuse and neglect. They and their families provide eloquent testimony in favor of continued court action. But there are other notable and essential gains that would result from such action. There is a new recognition of the meaning of individual rights within the field of human services and among the wider public. From a practical viewpoint, the United States Constitution had been for many little more than a vehicle for the experiment of Prohibition and for "taking the Fifth." There was little appreciation of the practical implications of the Bill of Rights as it must underlie human services. The court actions have resulted in a new and most welcome awareness in that respect.

The litigation has also clarified issues that reflected muddled professional thinking, such as making a child's admission to public school contingent upon the child's predicted capacity eventually to "return something tangible or intangible to the state" (Goldberg & Cruickshank, 1958). Finally, the court suits have resulted in a new appreciation of accountability, not only to the system, but to the person served. Inevitably, the results fall short of what is desired. Michael Lottman (1976) predicted the enforcement of the judicial decrees would be difficult. Such judicial decrees must face bureaucratic supervision as much as any new public policy, and system maintenance is as characteristic of public school administration as it is of the large, essentially autonomous, state institutions (see Dybwad, 1969a).

Furthermore, much of the implementation does not

---

[1] *See, e.g.,* Parham v. J.R., 442 U.S. 584 (1979); Kentucky Ass'n for Retarded Citizens v. Conn, 510 F. Supp. 1233 (W.D. Ky. 1980), *aff'd*, 674 F.2d 582 (6th Cir. 1982), *cert. denied sub nom.,* Bruington v. Conn, 103 S. Ct. 457 (1982); Davis v. Hubbard, 506 F. Supp. 915 (N.D. Ohio 1980); Johnson v. Solomon, 484 F. Supp. 278 (D. Md. 1979); Eckerhart v. Hensley, 475 F. Supp. 908 (W.D. Mo. 1979); Halderman v. Pennhurst State School and Hosp., 446 F. Supp. 1295 (E.D. Pa. 1977), *aff'd*, 612 F.2d 84 (3d Cir. 1979), *rev'd and remanded*, 451 U.S. 1 (1981), *on remand*, 673 F.2d 645 (3d Cir.), *cert. granted*, 102 S. Ct. 2956 (1982).

rest with the court. If the individual education plan (IEP) presents practical problems, it is up to the profession and the administration to work out a reasonable solution rather than suggesting that judicially imposed safeguards for children with handicaps are beyond the capacity of the public schools. In other words, the difficulties in implementing judicial decrees must be shared by administrators, professional workers, legislators, and last but by no means least, the affected individuals, as well as their families and their advocates to assure the protection of individual rights in a democracy.

To be sure, there had been at times poor judgment, too much rigidity, and undue delay, but overall the past 10 years have been very productive and we, the practitioners in the field of human services, owe a debt of gratitude to the courts and the attorneys who have fought valiantly so that others may have a more decent, dignified, and richer life.

CHAPTER 31
FROM FEEBLEMINDEDNESS TO SELF-ADVOCACY

*Excerpt from a presentation at the 118th Annual Meeting of
the American Association on Mental Retardation, June 1994*

Another significant development in the 1970s was the beginning of the People First movement. About 25 years after the first parent groups developed in the 1940s, groups of what became known as self-advocates appeared in this country. To Oregon and Washington must go the credit as the original pioneers, but the movements spread quickly and gained from close contacts with Canadian groups. The name People First emanated from this interaction.

There is no doubt that the initiative for this movement came from Sweden, where Bengt Nirje, well-known for his pioneering writing on the normalization principle, had discovered as ombudsman for the Swedish Parents Association that groups of young people in the Association's recreation program were far more capable of selecting and planning their activities than had seemed possible. At his suggestion, the Board allocated funds for some training sessions so as to enable these young people to take a more active part in programs which previously had been selected for them and to help them toward more skill in decision making. After Nirje had presented his experience with those pioneering Swedish self-advocates at a congress in Dublin, Ireland, his ideas were rather quickly picked up in England, Canada, and the United States. Already in 1973, a state ARC received a foundation grant supporting a project involving self-advocates. Conferences of self-advocates were beginning to be noted in the press and a slogan such as "Yes, we can" created a favorable climate.

In 1978 my wife was involved in planning the International League's Seventh World Congress in Vienna, and in conversation with others, the idea came up to have some self-advocates present and participate in that Congress. Dr. Clarence York of the Bancroft School and Community became interested and managed to arrange for a small group [of self-advocates] to travel to Vienna. At that time this seemed to be a formidable undertaking (an indication of our timidity) but all went well. There was a moment when we agonized in what special ways we should recognize at the Congress the presence of these young people, but then the point was made that nobody else was recognized by the Congress in a special way, so happily the idea was dropped. They came as regular Congress participants and were received as such.

Everything worked out so well that plans for the 1982 Congress of the International League which took place in Nairobi, Kenya, included from the beginning plans for a strong presence of an international group of self-advocates. Delegations from eight countries were present and, with the help of volunteer interpreters, the group of some 40 self-advocates developed in remarkably short time a sense of cohesion and team spirit.

One of their main tasks was to prepare for the fourth day of the Congress a plenary session to present their own ideas and feelings. And this they did, having selected eight from their midst to speak for them. An international audience of 700 people representing 65 countries listened and in the second half of the session had an opportunity to engage the eight self-advocates for an unrehearsed discussion.

For most of the audience, it was a startling revelation to see and hear people considered incompetent to speak so well for themselves and respond to challenging questions, at times with a good sense of humor.

At the League's next Congresses in 1986 in Rio de Janeiro and in 1990 in Paris, there was an ever-increasing participation of self-advocates and some of them by this time were quite critical of what they saw as inadequate consideration of their needs as Congress participants.

Meanwhile, the People First movement had their own International Congresses in 1984 in Washington State, in 1989 in London, England, and in 1993 in Toronto, Canada, quite a remarkable achievement considering how long it took AAMR [American Association on Mental Retardation] to move into the international field.

The Toronto Congress was for me a very moving experience beginning with an evening opening session with a long procession of the flags of the more than 30 participating countries. During the Congress, most speakers and most moderators came from the People First ranks, and sessions were organized to allow a maximum of participation. Keynote speeches each morning were limited to 10 minutes, something AAMR might well consider to adopt for its own meetings where often, after 45 minutes of listening, you wonder what the keynote really was. For those not yet used to large conference meetings, there were in Toronto many small discussion groups, limited in size and with no "outsiders" present.

But most impressive for an old-timer like me was the sight of a large hotel ballroom with more than 1,000 conference participants seated at dinner tables quietly having a meal. Of course the proper comment is "And why not?" But that is precisely why I began my presentation with the grim and, in retrospect, most painfully embarrassing realities of past decades.

Forty-five years ago, Mildred Thompson as AAMD [American Association on Mental Deficiency; forerunner of AAMR] president concluded that it would not be desirable, as had been suggested, to have the newly organized parent groups join AAMD under whatever arrangements. I am sure if Mildred Thompson could be here today, she would be pleased to observe that among the participants at this conference are a considerable number of self-advocates, not only speaking for themselves, but representing their own national organization, duly incorporated, and recognized as a nonprofit voluntary association about to have its first convention under its new name Self Advocates Becoming Empowered.

My purpose for this presentation was to highlight the importance of this new organization, the wisdom and dedication of its leadership, and its potential contribution toward changing traditional patterns in the community. It is for that reason that I started out with the dark days of the 30s and 40s, when the most basic human rights were denied to those who now rightly claim to have achieved not just personal but also organizational independence.

So allow me a somewhat unusual but well-reasoned request: Please join me in applauding the leadership and members of Self Advocates Becoming Empowered.

Good luck to you, Nancy and Roland and T. J. and all the others. You have come a long way, but there is quite a journey still ahead of you.

As for the rest of us, there lies a tough task ahead because, let us be honest, we are not as ready to face the challenge brought to us by the self-advocacy movement as our policy statement on self-determination may suggest. Innumerable obstacles are in the way—job descriptions, regulations, administrative routines, legalistic reasoning, and, yes, liability and other administrative safeguards—they all are apt to interfere with our good intentions. But as always, I am an optimist. I rejoice how far we have been allowed to travel, and I have no doubt that the journey will go on.

CHAPTER 32
LEADERSHIP IN SELF-ADVOCACY

Excerpt from a presentation, "From Eglantyne Jebb to Barbara Goode: A Historical Perspective on Human Rights for Persons With Mental Handicap," to the International Conference on Human Rights for Persons With Mental Handicap, Prague, Czech Republic, September 1997

What I have been reporting about the self-advocacy movement has been rather positive, and you might ask: "Does this give too positive a picture?" My friend Bernard Carabello is one who indeed sees substantial problems. A former resident of the ill-famed institution of Willowbrook in New York State, he had led a dreary, ugly life until a journalist intruded into the institution with a film camera. Carabello was one of the very few people in the institution who provided genuine aid to the newspaper man, revealing to him conditions not even the camera of the journalist would or could reveal. He was helped to gain his freedom, and became active in self-advocacy. A few years ago, he had this to say about what challenges still had to be met:

> There is still much work that has to be done before people with developmental disabilities are truly seen as capable human beings. Much more federal and state legislation is needed to ensure that the gains made thus far will not be eroded or erased by political or economic pressures. And within the field of self-advocacy, many questions remain unanswered. Until these questions are resolved the movement will remain in its infancy and will not be able to proceed. Some of these questions are:
>
> - Who are the leaders of the self-advocacy movement, and whom do they represent?
> - Are they people with disabilities?
> - Are the self-advocates really making the decisions for their groups, or are advisors—inadvertently or consciously—influencing the decisions of the group members?
> - How much are self-advocates used for agency needs that is, groups being formed only to meet federal requirements for consumer participation, and never given any real voice in influencing agency policy or direction?
> - How many self-advocates sit as members on agency Board of Directors, or are in actual paid positions such as executive directors of self-advocacy organizations?
> - Where and how do advisors use the self-advocacy movement for agency gains at the expense of the self-advocates' individual work and ideas?
> - Are people with disabilities only allowed to be "self-advocates," or can they be "advocates" as well?

His points are well-taken, and lead us to the important question: How can we make sure that self-advocates are well-prepared for the tasks facing them? The answer lies to a considerable extent in an area that has been largely neglected, namely adult education such as is provided in folk high schools or community colleges. It is there that self-advocates can learn how to speak (and think) clearly and effectively, how to write a story for a newsletter (or even edit one!), how to participate in a public debate, how to give testimony before a committee of the legislature, and how to write a letter that clearly conveys a message, such as a letter to a local newspaper.

And then there is a need to know a computer, or a word processor, but let me be frank: I am an 88-year-old fogy who does not know how to use them, but I know 7-year-old children with Down syndrome who can and do use them. Next in line is a need to know about your government, local, state, and national, and the different branches of government, legislative, administrative, and judicial.

It is not enough to know a problem; you must know somebody. You must know what person in what office to contact to get help. As an inveterate optimist, I have the confidence that in country after country, we will be able to observe the evolution of a leadership in self-advocacy that can face the weaknesses as expressed by Carabello.

A tangible example is a publication entitled *The Beliefs, Values, and Principles of Self Advocacy* (International League, 1996). The authors are seven self-advocates, from seven different countries, who were enabled by the generosity of the Swedish Parent Association, to meet twice for 3 days of planning and writing, first in Utrecht, Holland, and the second time in London, England. Their book should be read unquestionably, not only by every self-advocate, but by anyone who wants to understand this movement. The chairman of this group was none other than our friend Barb Goode. One of the members of the group was Ake Johanssen of Sweden, a man who had been forced to live in an institution for 32 years until he literally liberated himself. He has since related his life story to a writer, who has published it under the title *Ake's Book,* (Lundgren, 1994), a most moving testimonial of this man's maturity and compassion, as witnessed by this quote by him, "Human dignity is not a matter of intelligence. The important thing is to give the love and knowledge you have to your fellow human beings."

Let me end with a rather personal story. In the early 1960s, my wife and I worked on an international mentally handicapped assignment. Among the 30-odd countries we visited was Poland. There we met Mr. and Mrs. Garlicki, who with the approval of the authorities, had organized parents of mentally handicapped children in Poland. We had several visits to their home and met their daughter Joanna, a young woman with Down syndrome who led, for those days, a most unusually constructive and productive existence, helping with a lot of house cleaning, cooking, and also shopping, and volunteering in the afternoons in a nearby orphanage. She so impressed us that we wrote about her in an article published in the *International Child Welfare Review*. Last year, there was held in Warsaw, Poland, a conference on human rights with participation from many European countries. On the second day, a group of Polish self-advocates joined the conference, and there, after 30 years, I met again Joanna Garlicki, who was chair of the group of Polish self-advocates. A deeply moving experience that personified for me, in a striking way, the growth of the self-advocacy movement from its modest beginnings.

Chapter 33
Societal Perspectives: Where Do We Go From Here?

From "Societal Perspectives: Where Do We Go From Here?" in Aubrey Milunsky (Ed.),
Coping With Crisis and Handicap (pp. 309-315), 1981, New York: Plenum Press, reprinted with permission

Societal perspectives are to a considerable extent related to societal perceptions, and I think it is fair to say that there is a reciprocal relationship. A change in societal perception of persons with handicap will of necessity result in new societal perspectives, but it is equally obvious that once these new perspectives have been implemented, the changed circumstances of societal life will cause us to form changed perceptions.

On the broadest societal scale in the world community, the programmatic implementation of a succession of resolutions by the United Nations will demonstrate this interrelationship. Following one of the most destructive decades in human history, characterized by the Holocaust and a brutal war and culminating in the disasters of Hiroshima and Nagasaki—a decade that resulted in the enslavement, the maiming, and the death of millions of people—the United Nations came into being. One of its first major accomplishments was to create a new societal perspective with the Universal Declaration of Human Rights.

That was in 1948, and it was exactly at that time that in countries around the globe, parents of the handicapped children began to rise up and demand from society a better life and a greater acceptance for their children. It may seem strange to link together these two developments, but the only clue I have found in trying to determine what caused the sudden uprising of these parents in so many different parts of the world is that, side by side with the incredible human destruction during and after the war, we also observed incredible feats of human reconstruction. The key issue of the emerging rehabilitation and habilitation movement was a belief in the value and dignity of all human beings, their right to life, to liberty, and to security of person.

This first very broad Declaration of Human Rights was followed in 1959 by the Declaration of the Rights of the Child, and in that Declaration there was specific mention of the child with a handicap. But what was far more significant was the implied shift in societal perspectives as far as the children's role and rights were concerned. For some of our contemporaries the significance of this second Declaration may not be so obvious unless and until they realize that even in our own country in the early years of this century attempts to curb child labor, through the introduction of legislation that would stop the maiming of children at work in factories, was repeatedly judged unconstitutional. Children were deemed not to have *any* rights.

But what distinguished, in our context, the Declaration of the Rights of the Child from the Declaration on Human Rights is that it specifically prescribes that the child who is physically, mentally, and socially handicapped shall be given the special treatment, education, and care required by his particular condition.

It was slightly more than a decade later, when, in December 1971, the United Nations General Assembly adopted the Declaration on the Rights of Mentally Retarded Persons, and I emphasize this last word—*persons*. This Declaration, which spelled out in detail the general and specific rights that must be granted to persons with mental retardation, served as a precursor to a broad Declaration on the Rights of Disabled Persons, adopted by the United Nations in 1975. And not only United Nations personnel, but also national governments throughout the world, including the government of the United States, have planned a program of action and public information and education for the International Year of Disabled Persons, 1981.

I have gone far afield, but I wanted to lay a good foundation for the next point—my perception of the changing societal perspectives for persons with handicaps in our own country. Programs for children and adults with handicaps in the United States were characterized for many years by a "yes, but…" attitude. They were exclusionary programs and, to use the language of our vocational rehabilitation bureaucrats, were open only to those deemed "feasible." As a result, very often those persons most urgently in need of help would not receive it, and this was particularly true with the individuals who have been the subject of our discussions here today.

The 1950s and 1960s witnessed in our country ever more effective work on the part of organizations interested in the handicapped and increasingly, by persons with handicaps themselves, although at first primarily those with physical or perceptual handicaps. And then in the 1970s we came upon a decade of unprecedented change in societal perspectives. I say unprecedented because it surely was the first time that a major societal institution, namely the Judicial System, responded in broad terms to the needs of yet another minority group, those with severe handicaps who either suffered severe discrimination in school or even exclusion from it and those who were imprisoned by society in institutions where they were exposed (and even today are still exposed) to rampant abuse and neglect, often resulting in serious deterioration and physical harm.

From Alabama to Michigan, from Maine to Kentucky, in more than a score of cases, judges in Federal District Courts came to the conclusion, based on sworn testimony, that societal perspectives in the field of handicap needed a thorough overhaul. It is an interesting commentary on society in general and on the professional community specifically that it took courts of law to point up the extreme abuses in testing and classifications of children with disabilities and, yet more importantly, to point up that there is no child who is uneducable, that there is no child, no matter how severe his impairment, who cannot grow and develop. It was indeed a fascinating development in our society that a federal judge in California had to explain to the professional community in his state that if one uses an English-language *Stanford-Binet Test* with children from Spanish-speaking homes, the results are most likely inconclusive.

Added to the impact of this judicial activity came a legislative revolution, the Rehabilitation Act of 1973, the Developmental Disability Amendments of 1975 and 1978, and also in 1975, Public Law 94-142, the Education for All Handicapped Children Act, all stressing the importance of serving persons with severe handicap. Together, these three laws represent in effect a new congressional perspective on the problems of handicap and indeed, a far reaching new societal perspective.…

Today, not 100, not 10,000 but hundreds of thousands of substantially handicapped individuals walk on the streets or get about in wheelchairs, shop at supermarkets, go to movies, use buses and street cars, and go to ball games and playgrounds—places where they never used to be seen—and yet the number of untoward incidents is minimal. We have here a clear example of how a new perception, observing one's handicapped neighbors, leads to a readiness to accept new societal perspectives. To use an old adage, "Seeing is believing."

So far, I have presented what some may feel is an almost euphoric picture. Are there no impediments to the implementation of these new perspectives? There are and very formidable ones at that. And, strange as it seems, I see these major impediments as originating with my professional colleagues in psychology, social work, medicine, and the other so-called helping professions, and I would add the somewhat risky generalization that the higher the academic training my colleagues may have enjoyed, the more they are apt to impede persons with severe handicaps individually and collectively, by restrictive views, by a low level of expectation, and by a refusal to accept their educational or rehabilitation potential. I am well aware that these are grim words, but I think, with noble exceptions which always exist, by and large this has been the picture.

Let me be more specific: Over and over I have observed professional persons with advanced academic training, who become not just uncomfortable, but actively angry and even hostile when they are confronted with substantial achievements of persons whom they consider as incapable of making progress....

A small group of rather well-known academicians and administrators recently prepared for a federal court a position paper in which they sternly recommend continued incarceration of most of the more severely handicapped persons now in our retardation institutions. They specifically object to efforts to provide training and education, feeling that such a regime may constitute "cruel and inhuman treatment." Custodial care is what they see as appropriate for such individuals: kind custodial care that effectively segregates them as, in effect, subhuman. And it is not a very big step from custodial segregation to extermination.

There is another major impediment to the realization of the new perspectives I have presented. It is a political problem, long known by sociologists as "System Maintenance," a line of least resistance. The mental retardation institutions (which, of course, at least in the past, have housed persons with epilepsy, cerebral palsy, autism, and a variety of impairments that classified them as multiply handicapped) represent not only a past investment of hundreds of millions of dollars but are still today considered by legislators and politicians as ideal receptacles for new construction funds, again to the tune of hundreds of millions of dollars. In addition, they employ large groups of people who have come to feel that their employment in the institutions is a vested right. As a result, throughout this country, men, women, and children are kept imprisoned in these institutions not in consideration of their own needs but rather so that financial advantage will accrue to others.

But this is only one side of the story. Hundreds upon hundreds of millions of dollars are spent in this country to effect alterations and repairs in old out-moded institutional buildings without regard to cost effectiveness or minimal economic prudence in what can only be called an insane building spree, considering the cost per bed. And this insane waste of hundreds of millions of dollars to reconstruct unneeded institutional buildings in inappropriate locations is the major obstacle to the development of desperately needed, cost-effective community services.

Much as the general public can and does help with the adjustment of persons with mental retardation in the community, if only by allowing them to find their own way, the ordinary members of the general public are not likely to perceive the unholy conspiracy which perpetuates the institutional complexes, nor would they likely feel prepared to cope with it. A determined, unceasing campaign of convincing legislators of the intolerable fiscal burden they are asked to maintain is what is needed.

This campaign is making and will continue to make heavy demands on the associations for retarded citizens and related advocacy organizations. However, I predict that they will be supported with increasing effectiveness by a new phenomenon, the self-advocacy of persons with mental retardation and other developmental disabilities....

I join those who feel it is safe to predict that this new societal perspective will result in a new and more favorable perception of persons with mental retardation as fellow citizens, endowed with individual rights and capable of learning to contribute to the commonwealth—no longer just objects of pity and charity.

Biographical Sketch of Gunnar Dybwad

Dr. Gunnar Dybwad is professor emeritus of human development at the Heller School, Brandeis University. He served as senior staff member of the Center on Human Policy, Syracuse University, and visiting scholar at the G. Allen Rocher Institute, Toronto, Canada (formerly the National Institute on Mental Retardation).

He received his JD from the Faculty of Laws, University of Halle, Germany, and is a graduate of the New York School of Social Work. It was during the completion of his JD degree that he met his future wife, Rosemary Ferguson, who came to Germany as a graduate exchange student in sociology in 1933 through the German International Exchange Bureau. Dr. Dybwad's older sister worked for the Exchange Bureau and invited the exchange students to the Dybwad family home one weekend when Gunnar happened to be visiting his parents. Rosemary and Gunnar found an initial common interest in the English prison system; according to Gunnar, their "limited mutual knowledge" made them both feel a need to continue their exchange. At the end of her exchange term, the two collaborated in writing a request for Rosemary to stay an additional year. The request was so excellent that Rosemary was the first student ever to be allowed to extend her exchange.

In the spring of 1933, Gunnar went to Italy to collect information, and the following summer Gunnar wrote his dissertation on the "Theory and Practice of the Italian Penal System." Gunnar then joined Rosemary in Indianapolis, her family home, and in January 1934 Gunnar and Rosemary were married. They began their joint careers in the criminal justice field, working in the late 1930s predominantly in New Jersey and New York. Both Dybwads brought to their efforts an international vision of wide scope, based on their studies and on their extensive travels.

It was in New York that their focus began to shift toward the needs of people with disability. They began to notice many youngsters in the prison system who were not so much delinquents as they were people with significant cognitive limitations. Gunnar produced a major piece of writing on "The Problem of Institutional Placement for High Grade Mentally Defective Delinquents" which was presented in 1940 to the American Association on Mental Deficiency. From that point on, the Dybwad family interest gradually shifted to the conditions and needs of people with mental retardation and other disabilities, and their new careers were born.

From 1943 to 1951, Dr. Dybwad directed the child welfare program of the Michigan State Department of Social Welfare and subsequently served as executive director of the Child Study Association of America and of what was then the National Association for Retarded Children. From 1964 to 1967 he and Rosemary were codirectors of the Mental Retardation Project of the International Union for Child Welfare in Geneva, working as consultants throughout Europe and in Central and South America. This period included assignments in Spain and in Uruguay for the Rehabilitation Unit of the United Nations and consultations for the World Health Organization.

In this country Dr. Dybwad has served as consultant to President Kennedy's special assistant on mental retardation, to the U.S. Public Health Service, the U.S. Office of Education, the Social and Rehabilitation Service, the President's Committee on Mental Retardation, and numerous state governmental agencies. He was chairman of the Advisory Committee on Special Education to the Massachusetts State Board of Education and chairman of the Massachusetts Advisory Council on Planning, Construction, Operation, and Utilization of Facilities for the Mentally Retarded. From 1978 to 1982 he was president of the International Leagues of Societies for Persons With Mental Handicap, now known as Inclusion International.

He is fellow of the American Orthopsychiatric Association, the American Sociological Association, the American Public Health Association, and the American Association on Mental Retardation; a member of the Council for Exceptional Children; and honorary Associate Fellow of the American Academy of Pediatrics, from which he received in 1973 the C. Anderson Aldrich Award for his activities in the field of child development. In 1977 Temple University awarded him the honorary degree of Doctor of Humane Letters, and in 1984 he received the honorary degree of Doctor of Public Service from the University of Maryland.

Together with his wife, he has received awards for outstanding service from the American Association on Mental Deficiency, now American Association on Mental Retardation (1969, 1986, 1990, & 1997), the International League of Societies for the Mentally Handicapped (1972), the President's Committee on Mental Retardation (1977 & 1994), the National Association for Retarded Citizens (1978), the Massachusetts Psychological Association (1981), the International Association for the Scientific Study of Mental Deficiency (1981 & 1996), the Pike Institute of the Boston University School of Law, the Foundation for Dignity (Philadelphia), the Kennedy Foundation International Awards Program (1986), and the International Association for the Scientific Study of Intellectual Disabilities (1996).

Gunnar works in his extensive home gardens and continues to give visionary and challenging speeches all over the world. In recent years he has devoted a great deal of time and effort to establishing the Samuel Gridley Howe Library, located on the campus of the Fernald Developmental Center in Waltham, Massachusetts. The Howe Library is home to a remarkable collection of historical artifacts and documents detailing the evolution of services to people with mental retardation and other developmental disabilities, and it houses the personal collections of Dr. Irving Zola and Elizabeth Boggs. Dr. Dybwad continues to live outside of Boston in the house that he and his wife and family have shared since the early 60s. His house is an international bed and breakfast as well as his home; it is a rare day when Gunnar is not hosting one of his legion of friends and colleagues from around the world, or giving students and friends tea, coffee, and advice.

REFERENCES

Acton, N. (1971). Legislation and the rights of the disabled. *International Rehabilitation Review, 22*(1), p. 1.

Albizu-Miranda, C. (1970). Some historical and logical bases for the concept of cultural deprivation. In H. C. Haywood (Ed.), *Socio-cultural aspects of mental retardation.* New York: Appleton-Century-Crofts.

American Academy of Pediatrics. (1971). *The pediatrician and the child with mental retardation.* Chicago: Author.

American Medical Association. (1965). *Mental retardation: A handbook for the primary physician.* Chicago: Author.

American Medical Association. (1981). *Current opinions of the Judicial Council of the American Medical Association.* Chicago: Author.

Annas, G. J. (1979). Denying the rights of the retarded: The Phillip Becker case. *Hastings Center Report, 9* (6), 18-20.

Babula, M. (1991, September). Basics. *Down Syndrome News*, p. 85.

Baldwin, T. (1982). Infant death: Life and death in newborn special care units. *Connecticut Medicine*, 46-589-40L.

Bank-Mikkelsen, N. E. (1976). Patterns which are changing: Denmark. In R. Kugel & A. Shearer (Eds.), *Changing patterns in residential services for the mentally retarded* (Rev. ed.). Washington, DC: President's Committee on Mental Retardation.

Bernstein, R. (1985). Education for persons with disabilities, well worth the cost. *Newsletter of The Association for Persons with Severe Handicaps, 8* (3).

Biklen, D. (1988). Empowerment: Choices and change. *TASH Newsletter, 1* (6), 1.

Blatt, B., & Kaplan, F. (1966). *Christmas in purgatory: A photographic essay on mental retardation.* Boston: Allyn & Bacon.

Blatt, B., & Mangel, C. (1967, October 31). Tragedy and hope of retarded children. *Look.*

Cain, L. F., & Levine, S. (1963). *Effects of community and institutional school programs on trainable mentally retarded children.* Reston, VA: Council for Exceptional Children.

Caldwell, B., Bradley, R. H., & Elardo, R. (1975). Early stimulation. In J. Wortis (Ed.), *Mental retardation and developmental disabilities: An annual review.* New York: Bruner-Mazel.

Crocker, A., & Cushna, B. (1972, May). Pediatric decisions in children with serious mental retardation. *Pediatric Clinics of North America,* 19(2).

DeJong, G. (1983). Defining and implementing the independent living concept. In N. Crewe & I. Zola (Eds.), *Independent living for physically disabled people* (pp. 4-27). San Francisco: Jossey-Bass.

Duncan, P. M. (1860). *First report of the Eastern Counties Asylum for Idiots and Imbeciles.* Colchester, England: Essex and West Suffolk Gazette Office.

Dybwad, G. (1964a). Are we retarding the retarded? In G. Dybwad (Ed.), *Challenges in mental retardation.* New York: Columbia University Press.

Dybwad, G. (1964b). Medical needs of the displaced retarded child. In G. Dybwad (Ed.), *Challenges in Mental Retardation.* New York: Columbia University Press.

Dybwad, G. (1968). *The mentally handicapped child under five.* New York: National Association for Retarded Children.

Dybwad, G. (1969a). Action implications, U.S.A. today. In R. Kugel & W. Wolfensberger (Eds.), *Changing patterns in residential services for the mentally retarded.* Washington, DC: President's Committee on Mental Retardation.

Dybwad, G. (1969b). Prevention as a goal of social work: Is social work ready to meet the challenge of mental retardation? In *Proceedings—1968 Mental Retardation Institute.* Pittsburgh: Graduate School of Social Work, University of Pittsburgh.

Dybwad, G. (1973). Basic legal aspects in providing medical, educational, social, and vocational help to the mentally retarded. *Journal of Special Education, 7*(1), 39-50.

Dybwad, G. (1974). Whom do we call retarded? In President's Committee on Mental Retardation, *New Neighbors* (chap. 3). Washington, DC: President's Committee on Mental Retardation.

Dybwad, G. (1976, April). International view of mental retardation. In *Flash on the Danish National Service for the Mentally Retarded* (Publication No. 39). Copenhagen: Personnel Training School.

Dybwad, G. (1981a). Societal Perspectives: Where do we go from here? In A. Milunsky (Ed.), *Coping with crisis and handicap.* (pp. 309-315). New York: Plenum Press.

Dybwad, G. (1981b). The rediscovetry of the family. *Mental Retardation, 32*(1), 18-30.

Dybwad, G. (1983). Introduction. *Western New England Law Review, 5*(3), 323-336.

Dybwad, G. (1986). Ethical and legal problems in rehabilitation and medicine. In *The changing rehabilitation world: Into the 21st century* (pp. 10-15). New York: United Cerebral Palsy of New York City, Inc.

Dybwad, R. F. (1971). Organizational patterns of associations for the mentally retarded in developing countries. In *Proceedings of the second congress (1970) of the International Association for the Scientific Study of Mental Deficiency* (pp. 121-126). Warsaw: Polish Medical Publishers.

Edgarton, R. (1967). *The cloak of competence: Stigma in the lives of the mentally retarded.* Berkeley & Los Angeles: University of California Press.

Fabricant, M. (1988). Empowering the homeless. *Social Policy, 18*(4), 49-55.

Fletcher, J. (1972). Indicators of humanhood—a tentative profile of man. *Hastings Center Report, 5* (1).

Gallo, A. (1984). Spina bifida: The state of the art of medical management. *Hastings Center Report, 14.*

Goldberg, I. I., & Cruickshank, W. M. (1958). The trainable but noneducable: Whose responsibility? *National Education Association Journal, 47*(9), 622-623.

Gollay, E., Freedman, R., Wyngaarden, M., & Kurtz, N. R. (1978). *Coming back: The community experiences of deinstitutionalized mentally retarded people.* Cambridge, MA: A.B.T. Books.

Gross et al. (1983). Early management and decision making for the treatment of myelomeningocele. *Pediatrics, 72,* 4.

Grossman, H. J. (Ed.). (1973). *Classification in mental retardation.* Washington, DC: American Association on Mental Retardation.

Hansen, B. (1961, October). Let them be normal. *News and Notes.* Saginaw County (MI) Association for Retarded Children.

Heber, R. (1959). A manual on terminology and classification in mental retardation. *American Journal of Mental Deficiency,* 64 (Monograph Supplement).

Herr, S. (1984). The Phillip Becker case resolved: A chance for habilitation. *Mental Retardation, 22*, 1.

International League of Societies for the Mentally Handicapped. (1967). *Legislative aspects of mental retardation: Conclusions—Stockholm Symposium.* Brussels: Author.

International League of Societies for the Mentally Handicapped. (1969). *Symposium on Guardianship of the Mentally Retarded—Conclusions,* San Sebastian, Spain. Brussels: Author.

International League of Societies for the Mentally Handicapped. (1978). *Step by step: Guidelines on the implementation of the declaration on the rights of mentally retarded persons.* Brussels: Author.

International League of Societies for Persons With Mental Handicaps. (1996). *The beliefs, values, and principles of self-advocacy.* Cambridge, MA: Brookline Books.

Koch, R., & Dobson, J. C. (1971). *The mentally retarded child and his family.* New York: Bruner-Mazel.

Lottman, M. (1976). Enforcement of judicial decrees: Now comes the hard part. *Mental Disabilities Law Report, 69.*

Lundgren, K. (1994). *Åke's book.* Stockholm: Riksförbundet.

Massachusetts Department of Mental Health. (1973). *Home stimulation for the young developmentally disabled child.* Boston: Media Resource Center, Department of Mental Health.

Mills v. Board of Education of the District of Columbia, 348 F. Supp. 866 (D.D.C. 1972).

Mount, B., Beeman, P., & Ducharme, G. (1988). *What are we learning about bridge building?* Manchester, CT: Communitas.

Nirje, B. (1969). The normalization principle. In R. Kugel & W. Wolfensberger (Eds.), *Changing patterns in residential services for the mentally retarded.* Washington, DC: President's Committee on Mental Retardation.

Pearson, P. (1965, October). The forgotten patient: Medical management of the multiply handicapped retarded. *Public Health Reports, 80*, 915-918.

Pearson, P. (1968, November). The physician's role in diagnosis and management of the mentally retarded. *Pediatric Clinics of North America, 15*, 4.

Pennsylvania Association for Retarded Children. (1969, June). Resolutions of 19th annual convention. *Pennsylvania Message, 5*, 2.

Penrose, L. S., & Smith, G. F. (1966). *Down's anomaly.* London: Churchill.

Perske, R. (1972). The dignity of risk and the mentally retarded. *Mental Retardation, 19* (1), 24-27.

Perske, R. (1989). *Circle of friends: People with disability and their friends enrich the lives of one another.* Nashville: Abingdon Press.

President's Committee on Mental Retardation. (1967). *Mental Retardation 67: A first report to the president on the nation's progress and remaining great needs in the campaign to combat mental retardation.* Washington, DC: U.S. Government Printing Office.

President's Committee on Mental Retardation. (1968). *Mental Retardation 68: The edge of change.* Washington, DC: U.S. Government Printing Office.

President's Committee on Mental Retardation. (1970). *The six-hour retarded child.* Washington, DC: Author.

President's Committee on Mental Retardation. (1975). *The problem is growing. What are we waiting for?* (Reports of a conference on early intervention with high risk infants and young children, May 1974). Washington, DC: Author.

Proceedings of conference on Down's syndrome. (1969, November). New York Academy of Science.

Rappaport, J. (1984). Studies in empowerment: Introduction to the issue. *Prevention in Human Services, 3,* 1-7.

Roberts, E. (1982). Disabled Peoples' International: A symbol of determination. *Rehabilitation WORLD, 6,* 4.

Robertson, J. (1975). Involuntary euthanasia of defective newborns: A legal analysis. *Stanford Law Review, 27,* 213-269.

Rose, S. (1972). *Betrayal of the poor: The transformation of community action.* Cambridge, MA: Schenkman.

Sajón, R. (1965, October) *Legal and social development in mental retardation in Latin America.* Unpublished paper presented at the Inter-American Workshop on Mental Retardation, San Juan, Puerto Rico.

Sales, B., et al. (1982). *Disabled persons and the lone state legislative issues.* New York: Plenum Press.

Sarason, S. (1969). The creation of settings. In R. Kugel & W. Wolfensberger (Eds.), *Changing patterns in residential services for the mentally retarded* (pp. 341-357). Washington, DC: President's Committee on Mental Retardation.

Shaw, A. (1977). Defining the quality of life: A formula without numbers. *Hastings Center Report,* 7 (5), 11.

Shearer, A. (1984a). *Everybody's ethics: What future for handicapped babies?* London: Campaign for Mentally Handicapped People.

Shearer, A. (1984b). *Think positive! Advice on presenting people with mental handicap.* Brussels: International League of Societies for Persons With Mental Handicaps.

Skarnulis, E. (1976, August). *The residential assumptions.* Working paper for the NARC/ILSMH Symposium on Normalization and Integration: Improving the Quality of Life, Arlie, VA.

Skarnulis, E. (1979). Support, not supplant, the natural home. In *Home based services for children and families.* Springfield, IL: Charles C. Thomas.

Sundram, C. J. (1988). Regulation: Have we all gone mad? *Links, 18*(4), 11-14.

Terman, L. (1916). *The measurement of intelligence.* Boston: Houghton Mifflin.

United Nations Economic and Social Council. (1975, January). *Rehabilitation of disabled persons.* Report of the secretary-general to the Commission for Social Development. (Document E/CN.5/5000). New York: Author.

USA Today. (1985, April 25). p. A9.

Vail, D. J. (1966). *Dehumanization and the institutional career.* Springfield, IL: Charles C. Thomas.

Valera, R. (1983). Organizing disabled people for political action. In N. Crewe & I. Zola (Eds.), *Independent living for physically disabled people* (pp. 311-326). San Francisco: Jossey-Bass.

Whitten, E. (1957). Rehabilitation for independent living. *Journal of Rehabilitation, 23,* 4.

World Health Assembly. (1977, May). *Resolution 30.38.* (Document A30/VR13).

World Health Organization. (1976a). *The primary health worker: A working guide.* (Document HAD/74.5 rev.). Geneva: Author.

World Health Organization. (1976b, June). *Report of the group meeting on mental health and mental legislation, Cairo.* (Document EM/MENT/82). Alexandria: Author.

World Health Organization. (1977, April). *Mental retardation. Report by the director-general, 30th World Health Assembly.* (Document A30/15). Geneva: Author.

Young, W. (1969, April). Poverty, intelligence, and life in the inner city. *Mental Retardation, 70*(2), 24-29.